WHAT WOULD JESUS SAY ABOUT YOUR CHURCH?

Richard Mayhue

Christian Focus Publications

DEDICATION
To my special friend
John F. MacArthur, Jr.
whose love for Christ's church
is exceeded only by that of
the Chief Shepherd.

Richard Mayhue, Th.D. serves as Senior Vice President and Dean of The Master's Seminary in Sun Valley, California, USA. He has simultaneously been involved with both pastoring and training pastors for most of his over twenty years in ministry. Dr Mayhue has authored or edited ten books including *Rediscovering Expository Preaching*, *Rediscovering Pastoral Ministry* and *The Healing Promise*.

© 1995 Richard L Mayhue
ISBN 1-85792-150-X

Published by
Christian Focus Publications Ltd.
Geanies House, Fearn, Ross-shire,
IV20 1TW, Scotland, Great Britain.

Cover design by Donna Macleod

Printed and bound in Great Britain
by The Guernsey Press Co. Ltd, Vale, Guernsey, C.I.

Contents

The Seven Churches of Asia

Troas

Pergamum

Smyrna

Ephesus

Thyatira

Sardis

Philadelphia

Laodicea

Patmos

Athens

The Great Sea

0   100   200   300 km.

0   100   200 mi.

The Churches of Greece and the East

Black Sea

The Great Sea

Rome

Philippi

Thessalonica

Troas

Athens

Ephesus

Corinth

Antioch

Jerusalem

0   100   200 mi.

0   100 200 300 km.

Foreword

Pastors, like me, have spent the years of their ministry giving messages to the church. Sunday after Sunday in their own congregation and month after month in churches around the world, they have stood in the place of an undershepherd and called the people of God to sound doctrine and practice. They have written books, sent out radio broadcasts and made tapes geared to confront and instruct the church. Certainly, my ministry has had that relentless focus of endeavouring to impact the church to honour her Head, the Lord Jesus Christ. The messages I have brought have sometimes been wholeheartedly heeded, sometimes rejected, often tolerated and even treated with smiling indifference.

The church has brought the highs and lows of my life. It has been the source of my joys and sorrows. But what I have given a life to say to the church with conviction and concern can't begin to approach the 'concern for the churches' expressed by the Apostle Paul (2 Corinthians 11:28). His was a passionate devotion for which he sacrificed everything, including his life. For him, the church was the source of honour and dishonour, evil report and good report, sorrow and joy (see 2 Corinthians 6:8,10). But even his passion for the church bows in abject humility before the One who supremely loves the church – our Lord Jesus Christ. He said, 'I will build my church and the gates of Hades shall not overpower it' (Matthew 16:18). It is His church because He purchased it with His own blood (Acts 20:28).

In spite of such noble concern by Paul and faithfulness by our Lord, the church has done exactly what Paul prayed it would not do and has been repeatedly 'led astray from the simplicity and purity of devotion to Christ' (2 Corinthians

11:3). The body has wandered in deception and has both disobeyed and dishonoured her Lord. It seems preachers have exhausted their appeals with only modest success.

It is time for the church to listen directly to her Lord and He has spoken clearly, confrontively and compassionately. My thanks and yours should be to Richard Mayhue for taking us back to hear the audible voice of the Saviour as He pleads with His beloved.

John MacArthur
Pastor - Teacher
Grace Community Church
Sun Valley,
California

PREFACE

Sir Christopher Wren, the great architect of St. Paul's Cathedral in London, reportedly arrived at the construction site one day and inquired of three different workmen, 'What are you doing?' The first replied, 'I'm earning a meagre living to support my family.' The second said he was merely constructing another building.

The third had a grander view. 'I'm part of a magnificent project to build the world's most beautiful cathedral to the glory of God.' Unless we have the third worker's perspective, sooner or later we will lose our zeal for Christ's first love— the church. By neglect she will then fall into disrepair.

Even worse, another contemporary pitfall looms larger; it is possible to have a zeal for the church which is tragically misguided by the ways of the world rather than directed by Scripture. This danger finds modernity more appealing than God's Word when seeking solutions for contemporary problems that face the church. The church that is built this way will later be condemned by Christ, not commended.

When it comes to the late twentieth century evangelical church as a whole, techniques have unfortunately replaced truth, style has supplanted substance, convenience outdistances consecration, and modern church growth principles receive more attention than biblical church growth truth. Scripturally speaking, this is not Christ's intended state of affairs for His lovely bride—the church. This man-centred approach to the church spells out a gloomy future for what ought to be as bright as Christ's glory.

But what can be done to remedy this sad state of affairs? I join Isaiah in shouting, 'To the law and to the testimony' (Isaiah 8:20). Evangelicals desperately need to repent of their worldly approach to the church and return to the Scriptures. The church requires a fresh glimpse of her majestic Lord — Jesus Christ; and she needs to be re-acquainted with His revealed plan and purpose for the church as outlined in the Bible. She needs to be reminded that Christ will build His church His way.

Can you imagine Christ writing a letter directly to your church as He did to the seven churches of Asia (Revelation 2-3)? What would Christ say about twentieth century churches in light of what we know He wrote about first century churches? These studies are designed to help you know Christ's mind concerning the church in general and your church in particular.

Christ's thinking about the church has not changed from what was originally written in Scripture. Therefore, if the church is to regain her former glory, it must be through radical transformation by taking the church back to the basics as outlined in Scripture. Then we must all roll up our sleeves to engage in the hard work of restoring the church to her original beauty according to the biblical blueprint.

What Would Jesus Say About Your Church? starts with an assumed orthodox systematic ecclesiology. These studies quickly push beyond to the immediacy of 'applied' theology which can provide a biblical standard to determine how well or how terribly the church is being built.

I have written with pastors and lay people in mind, dealing in broad principles rather than trying to touch on every microscopic detail. The value of this study rests in its solid biblical content with the intent of knowing what Christ thinks about His churches. This volume goes forth with the author's prayer that Christ will use His Word to revitalize the church.

Now, before you begin, let me acknowledge the contributions of those without whose labours this book would not have been completed. Thank you to my wife 'B' and son Wade for sacrificially serving as computer whiz kids; to my son-in-law Michael Carson, a computer cartographer by profession, who contributed the maps; to my daughter Lee Carson and daughter-in-law Tracy McCormick who kept the household running; to Dennis Swanson, librarian at The Master's Seminary, for help in acquiring hard to obtain books and journal articles; to Drs. Irv Busenitz and Al Potter, colleagues at The Master's Seminary, who read the manuscript and made helpful improvements; to my grandson Iain who kept me young through the writing process; and to my great-grandfather Galbraith of Scottish ancestry whose prayers were answered by God in my conversion and call to ministry.

Richard Mayhue, Th.D.
The Master's Seminary
Sun Valley,
California

In each chapter, scripture references are given to prove each point. It is important that you look up each reference. After you have read a chapter, I would urge you to spend time considering the relevant questions found in the study section at the end of the book.

INTRODUCTION

'I Will Build My Church!'

'And also I say to you that you are Peter, and upon this rock I will build My church; and the gates of Hades shall not overpower it' (Matthew 16:18).

'Crossroads.' 'Transition.' 'Crisis.' 'Uncertainty.' 'Restlessness.' These unsettling words express the perception of many evangelicals regarding the immediate status of the church. Few would disagree that a call for redirection has come to the drifting evangelical church as the twenty-first century rapidly approaches. However, there is no current consensus on which route the church should take to get back on track.

Today's dilemma
In order to appreciate the confusion, consider John Seel's 1992 survey of twenty-five prominent evangelical leaders.[1] The leaders expressed their views on the general state of evangelicalism at the end of the twentieth century. Eight dominant themes emerged from their less-than-optimistic responses:

1. Uncertain identity—A widespread confusion over what defines an evangelical.

2. Institutional disenchantment—A perceived ministry ineffectiveness and irrelevance.

3. Lack of leadership—A lament over the paucity of spiritual leadership in the church.

4. Pessimistic about the future—A belief that evangelicalism's future hangs in the balance.

5. Growth up, impact down—A confusing paradox without immediate clear explanations.

6. Cultural isolation—A complete arrival of the post-Christian era.

7. Pragmatic response to problems—A drift toward unbiblical approaches to ministry.

8. Shift from truth-orientation ministry to market-response driven ministry—A redirection away from the eternal toward the temporal in order to be viewed as relevant.

For certain, the decisions made in this decade will reshape the evangelical church for much of the century to come. Thus, the future direction of the contemporary church is a pre-eminent concern. Unquestionably, the late twentieth-century church faces a defining moment. The real contrast in competing ministry models should not be the 'traditional' versus the 'contemporary' as commonly claimed, but rather the scriptural compared to the unscriptural.

'Re-engineering the Church' was the theme of a prominent 1994 pastoral leadership conference on how to prepare the church for the twenty-first century. As I read the conference brochure, my initial response was, 'Why re-engineer the church when God designed it perfectly in the beginning? Shouldn't we inspect the church first and replace only the defective portions? Wouldn't it be best to rebuild the demolished part according to the Builder's original plan? Who can improve on God's engineering?' I concluded that the solution is not re-engineering, but *restoration* to the perfect, original specifications of the divine Designer. The goal of any changes should be a return to the church's biblical roots.

An inspection of the existing church for areas of needed restoration should include such biblically oriented questions as:

Have we consulted the *Owner* (1 Corinthians 3:9)?

Do we have the permission of the *Investing Partner* (Acts 20:28)?

Are we dealing with the *original Builder* (Matthew 16:18)?

Does the church still rest on the *beginning Foundation* (1 Corinthians 3:11; Ephesians 2:20)?

Is the *first Cornerstone* still in place (Ephesians 2:20; 1 Peter 2:4-8)?

Are we using *approved building materials* (1 Peter 2:5)?

Do we employ the right *labourers* (1 Corinthians 3:9)?

Have we utilized the *appropriate supervisors* (Ephesians 4:11-13)?

Are the initial *standards of quality control* still in place (Ephesians 4:13-16)?

Are we continuing to work from the *original blueprint* (2 Timothy 3:16-17)?

Yesterday's promise

Before wildly plunging ahead to restore the church, we would do well by first looking back twenty centuries—to the beginning—at the greatest promise ever made on the church's behalf. The Author and Perfecter of our faith (Hebrews 12:2), also known as the Shepherd and Guardian of our souls (1 Peter 2:25), boldly asserted, '... I will build My church; and the gates of Hades shall not overpower it' (Matthew 16:18).

We might be persuaded to assume that a two thousand year old organization, such as the church, would be settled in her identity and purpose by now. However, this is an unwarranted assumption. Unless each succeeding generation returns to Christ's promise in Matthew 16 and to the New Testament building instructions, the church surely will deviate from God's original plan as has been proven conclusively over twenty centuries of church history.

If you seriously reflect on Christ's promise, a number of significant questions should arise:

To whom do we look when the church is in disrepair—Christ or man?

Who knows more about the current needs of the church—Christ or man?

Who can provide better for the church—Christ or man?

From whom did the original idea of the church come—Christ or man?

In whom rests the church's future hope—Christ or man?

Who built the church up until now—Christ or man?

Whom do we trust for future direction—Christ or man?

Who owns and sustains the church—Christ or man?

For whose glory does the church exist—Christ or man?

Who is the head of the church—Christ or man?

Because 'Christ' is the correct answer to each of these questions, we turn to Matthew 16:18 where Jesus delivers at least seven hallmark principles for building the church. No one should launch out in planning a new church or take on the risk of revitalizing a worn-out church until the defining truths of this Scripture have gripped one's heart and mind.

Tomorrow's hope

Hallmark 1
The initial characteristic involves a *permanent foundation*. Christ passionately pursued the lasting fruit of eternity. In His promise, He explicitly looked to an everlasting legacy. Jesus did not have in mind the temporary, the faddish, or the 'here today, gone tomorrow'. He pointed to the church as having a 'forever' relevance.

'I also say that you are Peter, and *upon this rock* I will build My church.' The foundation wasn't Peter, because Christ here distinguishes between a moveable rock/detached boulder (the basic meaning of Cephas and Peter) and the unshakeable, immovable foundation suitable for the church. The word Christ used for 'rock' means bedrock or mass of rock as used by the wise builder (Matthew 7:24-25).

What or who then is the rock? The Old Testament pictures

God as a rock in whom we find strength and refuge:

> There is no-one holy like the LORD,
>> Indeed, there is no-one besides Thee,
>> Nor is there any rock like our God (1 Samuel 2:2).

> The LORD is my rock and my fortress and my deliverer,
> My God, my rock, in whom I take refuge ... (Psalm 18:2).

> For who is God, but the LORD?
> And who is a rock, except our God? (Psalm 18:31).

Paul identifies Christ as the rock in the wilderness (1 Corinthians 10:4). Earlier in 1 Corinthians (3:11), the Apostle wrote, 'For no man can lay a foundation other than the one which is laid, which is Christ Jesus'.

Interestingly, one verse earlier Paul had claimed, 'I laid a foundation ...'. How did Paul 'lay' Christ as the foundation? Obviously, it had to be in his preaching of Christ (1 Corinthians 2:1-2). Now, if Paul's testimony of Christ is the foundation that no one else can lay, then it seems best to understand the 'bedrock foundation' of the church to be Peter's testimony of Christ, 'Thou art the Christ, the Son of the living God' (Matthew 16:16). Remember, Peter's declaration prompted Jesus' promise.

Since it is virtually impossible to separate the testimony of Christ from the reality of Christ, we can identify the 'rock' as Christ Himself in the fullness of His deity, His role as redeemer, and His headship in the church. Christ alone is the rock of redemption upon which the church is being built (Acts 4:11-12).

Hallmark 2

Secondly, Christ promised His *personal involvement*. '*I* will build My church.' We have not been left to the task alone. Christ is in us (Colossians 1:27), with us (Matthew 28:20), and amongst His church constantly (Revelation 1:12-13,20).

Paul told the Corinthian church, 'For we are God's fellow workers ...' (1 Corinthians 3:9). What a privilege to be partner's with Christ in building His church. How comforting to know He built the church before we arrived and He will continue to build long after we're gone. Christ's participation proves indispensable in raising up His church.

Hallmark 3

'I *will* build My church.' This is no idle dream about what might be. Christ's confident assertion guarantees that the church has a *positive expectation*. In times like these when the future of the church looks bleak and its condition uncertain, this powerful promise should buoy up our spirits. The church will be triumphant because Christ began building the church with the intention of completing her (Ephesians 5:26-27).

Hallmark 4

Jesus claimed that His church will have a *powerful advance*. 'I will *build* My church.' The church experienced an explosive beginning with 3,000 members being added on the first day (Acts 2:41). 'And the Lord was adding to their numbers day by day those who were being saved' (Acts 2:47).

What is contained in one mere sentence in Matthew 16 mushrooms into an expansive reality by the time of John's Revelation. Before the New Testament ends, churches existed across the face of the Roman Empire. They included locations like Rome, Corinth, Thessalonica, Philippi, Colossae, Laodicea, Ephesus, Galatia, Derbe, Lystra, Iconium, Antioch, Jerusalem, Crete, Cyprus, Smyrna, Pergamum, Thyatira, Sardis, Philadelphia, Caesarea, Berea, and Joppa. His building efforts continue to this very hour, everywhere in the world, just as He intended (Mark 16:15; Luke 24:47).

Hallmark 5
Christ bought the church with His own blood and therefore possesses the exclusive *paid-in-full ownership* of the church (Acts 20:28). 'I will build *My* church.' Christ is Lord; we are His servants (2 Corinthians 4:5). Paul writes to the believers in Rome, 'All the churches of Christ greet you' (Romans 16:16). Make no mistake about this—we do not (corporately or individually) have any ownership claim to the church. The church belongs uniquely to its Redeemer (1 Corinthians 3:23; 6:19-20). Christ is Head of the church (Ephesians 1:22; 5:23). The Chief Shepherd owns the flock that He leads (John 10:14-15).

Hallmark 6
'I will build My *church*.' For Christ, the church has a *people-centred priority*. The church comprises an assembly of people who have believed in Jesus Christ for eternal life (Acts 4:32). Jesus uses living stones—individual people—to build His church (1 Peter 2:5). The mandate of evangelization is to take the gospel to all the nations (Luke 24:47). The goal of edification is to present everyone complete in Christ (Colossians 1:28).

The Greek word translated 'church' literally means the congregation which has been called out. The New Testament pictures the church as made up of those who have been delivered out of the kingdom of darkness and transferred to the kingdom of Christ (Colossians 1:13). The Thessalonians had turned from idols to serve a true and living God (1 Thessalonians 1:9). The church has been called into fellowship with Jesus Christ (1 Corinthians 1:9). Christ has called His redeemed out of darkness into His marvellous light (1 Peter 2:9).

Hallmark 7

Jesus has *promised success* to the church. 'I will build My church; and *the gates of Hades shall not overpower it*.'

How is this success to be understood? In the Old Testament 'gates of' is used with Sheol (Isaiah 38:10) and death (Job 38:17; Psalms 9:13; 107:18), both referring to physical death. 'Death' is really the only enemy that could 'potentially' overpower and defeat the church since she is comprised of people who shall live, even if they die (John 11:25).

The writer of Hebrews encourages us to know that through death Christ rendered powerless him who had the power of death, that is the devil (2:14). Paul wrote this Christian victory song to the Corinthians:

> But when this perishable will have put on the imperishable, and this mortal will have put on immortality, then will come about the saying that is written, 'Death is swallowed up in victory. O Death, where is your victory? O Death, where is your sting?' The sting of death is sin, and the power of sin is the law; but thanks be to God, who gives us the victory through our Lord Jesus Christ (1 Corinthians 15:54-57).

When Christ builds the church these seven features will be identifiable:

1. Christ as the permanent foundation.
2. Christ's personal involvement.
3. Christ's positive expectation.
4. Christ's purpose of powerful advance.
5. Christ's paid-in-full ownership.
6. Christ's people-centred priority.
7. Christ's promise of success.

Who could possibly want to build the church any other way?

Christ's unfinished work

Theologians often speak of Christ's 'finished work' on the cross, referring to the work of redemption. Christ cried out on the cross, 'It is finished!' (John 19:30). Truly, Christ's sacrifice need not be offered again (Hebrews 7:27; 9:12). There is indeed the finished work of Christ.

However, more is in view for the church than just Christ's death and resurrection. Dr. Luke wrote his gospel concerning 'all that Jesus began to do and teach' (Acts 1:1). Just before ascending into heaven, Jesus told his disciples to be witnesses of Him to the remotest part of the earth (Acts 1:8). Reaching the lost with the gospel and then adding to the church daily until Christ returns is the unfinished work of building Christ's church.

What we are to be doing and how we are to do it in building Christ's church is the subject of this volume. By God-breathed, infallible revelation, Christ has communicated to us what He thinks about the church. The Scriptures particularize what He commends and specify what He condemns. No-one need ever be in doubt over how to go about the unfinished work of building Christ's church or what the outcome will be.

In the end, our work in building the church on behalf of

Christ will be acclaimed as valuable—the allusion to gold, silver and precious stones—or worthless—the allusion to wood, hay, and straw (1 Corinthians 3:12). The *quality* of each man's work will be tested by Christ in the end (1 Corinthians 3:13). Our eternal reward for service done on earth depends on building the church with biblical excellence in order to please Christ.

In the Academy Award-winning film *Chariots of Fire*, Eric Liddell, famed Olympian and missionary to China, conversed with his sister Jenny on a Scottish moor about the timing of his return to missionary work. His response remains etched in my memory. 'I believe that God made me for a purpose—for China—but He also made me fast. And when I run I feel His pleasure.'

Nothing will bring Christ greater pleasure than the building of His church. So, aim your life at the bull's-eye mark of His pleasure and you will never miss the spiritual target. You'll not be disappointed, and neither will Christ. Your heart will be filled with a great sense of commitment, as expressed by the words below, to build Christ's church his way.

> I rise up to worship, I stand to acclaim
> The King of all ages, Christ Jesus His name.
> I ask you, King Jesus, fulfill this desire,
> Ignite me and make me, a chariot of fire.
> Come rule all my life
> Lord Jesus Christ, be Master and King.
> Come rule all my life,
> Lord Jesus Christ, be my everything.[2]

PART ONE

THE CHURCHES OF ASIA

1

WHAT JESUS THINKS ABOUT HIS CHURCHES

I, John, your brother and fellow partaker in the tribulation and kingdom and perseverance which are in Jesus, was on the island called Patmos, because of the word of God and the testimony of Jesus. I was in the Spirit on the Lord's day, and I heard behind me a loud voice like the sound of a trumpet, saying, 'Write in a book what you see, and send it to the seven churches: to Ephesus and to Smyrna and to Pergamum and to Thyatira and to Sardis and to Philadelphia and to Laodicea.'

And I turned to see the voice that was speaking with me. And having turned I saw seven golden lampstands; and in the middle of the lampstands one like a son of man, clothed in a robe reaching to the feet, and girded across His breast with a golden girdle. And His head and His hair were white like white wool, like snow; and His eyes were like a flame of fire; and His feet were like burnished bronze, when it has been caused to glow in a furnace, and His voice was like the sound of many waters. And in His right hand He held seven stars; and out of His mouth came a sharp two-edged sword; and His face was like the sun shining in its strength.

And when I saw Him, I fell at His feet as a dead man. And he laid His right hand upon me, saying, 'Do not be afraid; I am the first and the last, and the living One; and I was dead and behold, I am alive forevermore, and I have the keys of death and of Hades.

'Write therefore the things which you have seen, and the things which are, and the things which shall take place after these things. As for the mystery of the seven stars which you saw in My right hand, and the seven golden lampstands: the seven stars are the angels of the seven churches, and the seven lampstands are the seven churches' (Revelation 1:9-20).

The New Testament pictures Jesus Christ in relationship to the church as Chief Shepherd (1 Peter 5:4), Bridegroom (Revelation 19:7), Head (Ephesians 5:23), Mediator (1 Timothy 2:5), High Priest (Hebrews 8:1), and Advocate (1 John 2:1). John adds to these and portrays Him as *Lord of the church* (Revelation 1:9-20).

The major theme of Revelation focuses on 'Christ Unveiled'. That's why the title given to Revelation in some versions of the Bible is 'The Revelation of Jesus Christ'. Revelation can easily be outlined around the person of Christ:

1. Christ's Glory (Revelation 1)
2. Christ's Churches (Revelation 2-3)
3. Christ's Future Plans (Revelation 4-22)

A teacher once asked a teen if he could summarize Revelation in one sentence. The young person shot back, 'Sure, that's easy.' Shocked but interested, the adult asked for the answer. 'Jesus wins,' he replied. Revelation affirmatively answers the question, 'Did Jesus keep His promise to build the church against which the gates of Hades would not prevail?'

I will build My church

Jesus does win and comes to rule the earth for 1,000 years (Revelation 19-20). Later, He eternally rules the new heaven and new earth (Revelation 21-22). But before His final victories over Satan (Revelation 6-20), He must build His church as He promised (Matthew 16:18).

In order to complete the project, Christ knew that some individual churches needed to be remodelled or even rebuilt. So He lovingly, but bluntly, wrote to seven churches in Asia Minor (Revelation 1:4, 11) assessing their condition.

Two of the churches received a glowing commendation from Christ with instructions to continue on (Smyrna and Philadelphia). The other five needed to roll up their sleeves and get to work to restore their original condition. Two of the five had major spiritual damage and deficiencies so they received nothing but condemnation (Sardis and Laodicea). The others (Ephesus, Pergamum and Thyatira) had much going for them but needed some remodelling; thus, Christ's comments to them include both commendation and condemnation.

Without a doubt, Revelation 2-3 gives us the greatest insights into what Christ values in His church and what He considers vile. These seven churches provide models to which we can compare our churches and answer the question, 'What does Christ think about our church?'

Seven cities—seven churches

Church tradition reports that John, the human author of Revelation, ministered at Ephesus in his latter years. It's not surprising then to see these letters addressed to Ephesus and six other surrounding cities within 100 miles of Ephesus, to the north and east. Undoubtedly, John, who was now in his nineties, ministered to each of these churches in his travels. Each of the churches had existed for about forty years and would have comprised the second or third generation of believers since their beginning.

All of the churches were located on one major highway system. This most likely explains how they came into existence and why Christ selected these seven, for they could be reached easily by courier. Each of the cities also served as the centre of a postal district.

What do these churches represent? Some say they prophetically represent seven periods of church history ranging from John's day until Christ comes. While this is possible, a better explanation is that these churches most likely represent seven different kinds of churches that have existed during any one period of church history including today. Consider these strong reasons for favouring this approach.

1. These seven real churches existed at the same time.

2. Revelation never hints that these churches represent stages of church history.

3. A careful analysis of church history does not parallel these seven churches.

4. On eight occasions Revelation reports that these materials are for the churches, not that they picture periods of church history (2:7; 2:11; 2:17; 2:29; 3:6; 3:13; 3:22; 22:16).

5. All seven kinds of churches have existed in each period of church history.

The ultimate issue
Although the Roman judicial system had at one time been a safe haven for Christians being persecuted by the Jews (compare Paul's appeal to Caesar in Acts 25:10-11), by the time John wrote the Book of Revelation the church had endured tremendous tribulation from the government.

He writes: 'I, John, both your brother and fellow partaker in the tribulation and kingdom and perseverance which are in Jesus, was on the island called Patmos because of the word of God and the testimony of Jesus' (Revelation 1:9).

The ultimate issue focused on Lordship. When John wrote, Caesar worship prevailed whereby every citizen in the Empire had to appear annually before a magistrate to worship Caesar by burning incense and saying, 'Caesar is Lord.' Emperor Domitian (AD 81-96) demanded to be worshipped as

God and addressed as, 'Dominus et deus', that is, Lord and God.

No wonder that John experienced tribulation because of the Word of God and the testimony of Jesus. The Word of God declares that to worship someone other than God is idolatry (Exodus 20:3-6; 1 John 5:20-21) and the testimony of Jesus pointed to His deity (John 1:1). The echoes of Joshua's age-old maxim still reverberated, 'Choose for yourselves today whom you will serve' (Joshua 24:15).

John would shortly portray the true King receiving true worship in heaven (Revelation 4-5). Jesus Christ is declared to be 'King of Kings and Lord of Lords' (Revelation 19:16). The entire book of Revelation reaffirmed what Scripture already had declared about Christ's Lordship over government and history; it also revealed some new details to bolster the faith of these beleaguered saints.

Every generation faces the question of Lordship. We do well to remember that whatever or whomever vies for our allegiance does so in opposition to Christ's true Lordship: 'As you therefore have received Christ Jesus the Lord, so walk in him' (Colossians 2:6).

So John presents Jesus Christ as Lord of the church and the only one from whom lasting peace comes (Revelation 1:4). Ultimately, John falls at Christ's feet as a dead man in reverence and worship (Revelation 1:17).

Christ's glory

After a preface (1-3) and a specific introduction to Revelation for the reader (4-8), John reports his sighting of the majestic glory of Christ (9-20). While a prisoner on Patmos, he heard a loud voice on the Lord's day, which would be the first day of the week, the day on which Christians worshipped Christ in celebration of His resurrection—His victory over death. The voice belonged to the triumphant Lord Jesus Christ (1:17-18).

John turned and saw Christ in the midst of His churches, resplendent in all of His glory. Christ will not again show His glory in full like this until He returns to the earth at His second coming (Revelation 19:11-16).

If John's imprisonment had planted seeds of doubt regarding Christ's Lordship over the church or concern for His church, this appearance quickly uprooted them. Undoubtedly, John had appealed prayerfully to Christ for help with the churches, most of whom were already faltering. Nothing could have been more shocking than for Christ to appear before John in his imprisonment and provide a personal word for each of the seven churches. John might have been imprisoned but neither the written Word of God nor the living Word can be confined.

Christ's attire, appearance, and appeal each serve to bolster John's faith and reaffirm God's truth. We can relive John's experience with the same expected outcome in our lives through his inspired record of this spectacular but altogether startling visit by the Lord of the church.

Christ's attire (1:13)
He wore a robe reaching to His feet and a golden sash across His chest. It does not point to Christ in His high priestly role since the sash is not blue, purple and scarlet (Exodus 39:29). Neither does His attire point to Him as King since He wears no crown.

Christ's appearance reminds us of the messenger in Daniel 10:5-6:

> I lifted my eyes and looked, and behold, there was a certain man dressed in linen, whose waist was girded with a belt of pure gold of Uphaz. His body also was like beryl, his face had the appearance of lightning, his eyes were like flaming torches, his arms and feet like the gleam of polished bronze, and the sound of his words like the sound of a tumult (see also Daniel 12:6 and Revelation 15:6).

He came dressed as a prominent person with an important message. In other words, Christ appeared in His prophetic role with the Word of God concerning His present plans for the church and His future plans for the world (cf. Revelation 1:19). His apparel demanded a hearing. Even though He appeared like 'a son of man', i.e. a human being, that which follows clearly identifies this prophetic messenger as none other than the Godman—Jesus Christ.

Christ's appearance (1:14-16)
His head and His hair were white like white wool, like snow. The 'Ancient of Days' image (Daniel 7:9) couples with white hair, the outward sign of wisdom (Proverbs 16:31; 20:29), to picture Christ's *eternal wisdom*. The one in whom is hidden all the treasure of wisdom and knowledge (Colossians 2:3), the one who is the wisdom of God (1 Corinthians 1:24, 30) has arrived. We need to seek only Christ since He alone can provide eternal wisdom to address the problems of the church. It's no wonder, then, that each letter contains the admonition, 'He who has an ear, let him hear ...' (2:7, 11, 17, 29; 3:6, 13, 22). Let him learn eternal wisdom from the Lord of the church.

His eyes were like a flame of fire (cf. Daniel 10:6). Eyes represent knowledge. God's eyes, representing His *omniscience* (knowing all things), remind us that God sees the world completely (2 Chronicles 16:9) and looks where men can't, on the human heart (1 Samuel 16:7).

So nothing in the church, either good or bad, has been hidden from Christ's sight and knowledge. The intense light of Christ's eyes penetrates the greatest darkness that exists in the church. His gaze saw the lie of Ananias and Sapphira (Acts 5:1-11) and knew all about the moral compromise in Thyatira (2:18). Because of this, every one of Christ's letters says, 'I know' (2:2, 9, 13, 19; 3:1, 8, 15). Christ knows all—that which He commends and that which He condemns.

His feet were like burnished bronze when it has been caused to glow in a furnace (cf. Daniel 10:6; Ezekiel 1:7). Feet represent defeat and judgment to those on whom they tread (cf. Psalm 110:1; Revelation 14:17-20). The fire has tempered the feet with strength and purified them for judgment. With uncorrupted purity Christ is strong enough to conquer sin in the church and pure enough to judge it. Christ will not permit a prolonged pattern of libertine living in the church. He will step in to purge his bride of corrupting sin and perfect her in His holiness.

His voice was like the sound of many waters (cf. Psalm 29:3-9; Ezekiel 1:24). Christ's tumultuous voice represents His *omnipotence*. When the glory of God appeared, His voice was like the sound of many waters (Ezekiel 43:2). Nothing will be too hard for Christ in the church (Jeremiah 32:17) and Christ's power will compensate for human weakness (2 Corinthians 12:9). The church is built by Christ's power, not our strength (Matthew 16:18).

In His right hand He held seven stars (cf. Psalm 98:1). Christ's right hand represents prominent power or *sovereign authority*. John must have thought back to the Galilean breakfast when Jesus said that, 'All authority has been given to Me in heaven and on earth' (Matthew 28:18). His authority demands the obedience of both shepherd and sheep. We must obey God not men (Acts 5:29). Therefore, unlike the churches at Ephesus (2:1) and Sardis (3:1), we can conduct the affairs of the church with the spiritual authority of Christ.

Out of His mouth came a two-edged sword (cf. Isaiah 11:4; Revelation 19:15,21). This was the primary offensive weapon of war used by the Roman soldiers to secure a *certain victory*. Christ will fight on behalf of His church and win. Unlike Pergamum (2:12, 16), we can fight the good fight with the eternal prospect of victory (1 Corinthians 15:57).

His face was like the sun shining in its strength (cf. Exodus 34:29-35; Ezekiel 43:2). John had not seen this level of glory since the Mount of Transfiguration (Matthew 17:2). This same glory blinded Paul on the road to Damascus (Acts 9:3; 22:6; 26:13). Christ's glory will ultimately be the illumination of eternity (Revelation 21:23; 22:5). Christ's presence in the church now is a *majestic glory* to behold because He is light and in Him is no darkness at all (1 John 1:5). One day we will taste His glory when the saints shine forth as the sun in the Kingdom of their heavenly Father (Matthew 13:43).

If we were suddenly and unexpectedly exposed to the vividness of Christ, like John, what would we do? If we simultaneously could see Christ's eternal wisdom, omniscience, uncorrupted purity, omnipotence, sovereign authority, certain victory and majestic glory, what would we do? I'm sure we would respond like John and fall at His feet in awe and worship (1:17). The church needs a fresh glimpse of Christ's majesty and power.

Christ's Appeal (1:17-18)

John was not to be frightened by Christ's presence, but rather comforted and encouraged with His words and reassuring touch (1:17). The Lord of the church reminded John of three truths about Himself which would dispel any remaining discomfort.

I am the first and the last (cf. Isaiah 41:4; 44:6; 48:12-16). This speaks of Christ's self-sufficiency. He lacks nothing to complete what He began building in the church. Regardless of how helpless John might have been on Patmos or how hopeless the church might be without him, Christ is sufficient for all. So complete is Christ that later He says, 'I am the Alpha and the Omega, the first and last, the beginning and the end' (Revelation 22:13).

I am the living one; and I was dead, and behold I am alive for evermore. The ultimate authentication of Jesus Christ as the true builder of the church rests in His resurrection (Romans 1:1-6; 10:9; 1 Corinthians 15:1-3). The gates of Hades or death will not prevail over the victorious completion of the church.

I have the keys of death and Hades. Christ will put all enemies under His feet, including death and Hades (1 Corinthians 15:26). They will be thrown into the lake of fire because Christ has the key of authority over them. Death will not rob Christ of even one living stone in the building of His church. His divine authority will subdue even the most persistent enemy. Every one of God's elect, all of whom Satan tried to murder with sin, will be rescued by Christ's victory at the cross. Not even the gates of Hades will prevail over the church (Matthew 16:18).

Lord of the church

The church serves as the central theme of Revelation 1-3. 'Church' appears 17 times in Revelation; 16 of those are in Revelation 1-3—the final time at Revelation 22:16. Of the

numerous symbols used in Revelation 1, only those with
direct reference to the church and which do not have Old
Testament precedent are explained. Revelation 1:20 elabo-
rates on the 'lampstands' of 1:12-13 in whose midst Christ
stands and the 'seven stars' held in Christ's hand at 1:16. They
portray the centrality of Christ in His church.

Lampstands

Revelation 1:13 pictures Christ standing in the middle of
seven golden lampstands. The seven lampstands represent the
seven churches to which Christ is about to write (1:20). This
portrayal of Christ in the midst of the lampstands signifies His
presence among his churches, reminding us of Christ's promise to the disciples, 'Lo, I am with you always, even to the end
of the age' (Matthew 28:20), and telling of the high importance the church plays in Christ's thinking.

Note that the lamps are made of gold, the most valuable
metal known to mankind. It's important here to remember that
the church is made up of people not buildings. So the gold of
the lampstands represents the high value of humanity in the
economy of Christ. The 'gold' of the church was purchased
with something more valuable than gold—'with precious
blood, as of a lamb unblemished and spotless, the blood of
Christ' (1 Peter 1:19).

Lampstands serve as a source of light. So it is that the
church exists to light up a dark world. Christ came to be the
light of the world (John 1:9). The church is made up of people
who have been delivered from the domain of darkness and
now qualify to share in the inheritance of the saints in light
(Colossians 1:12-13). The church is thus commanded to
'walk as children of light' (Ephesians 5:8) and to 'Let your
light shine before men in such a way that they may see your

good works, and glorify your Father who is in heaven'
(Matthew 5:16). The emphasis here is on the church's responsibility to walk in a manner worthy of Christ's call (Ephesians
4:1; Colossians 1:10).

Stars

The seven 'stars' are the 'messengers' of the seven churches.
Most English translations use 'angel' instead of 'messenger'
to translate the Greek word *angelos*. However, it is better to
use the most general sense of this word, i.e. 'messenger', and
then let the context interpret its meaning.

'Star' in the Bible can refer to many things such as an actual
star (Revelation 6:13), demons (9:1), humans (12:1), Christ
(22:16) or angels (Job 38:7). It was common in ancient
literature for 'star' to represent an important person (Daniel
12:3). We even have our own 'stars' and 'superstars' today.

Angelos can refer to good angels (Revelation 5:11) or evil
angels (Matthew 25:41). Frequently in the New Testament it
is also used of human messengers (Matthew 11:10; Mark 1:2;
Luke 7:24; James 2:25).

With this in mind, there are three reasonable interpreta-
tions of 'star'. Some say it refers to the 'attitude' of the church.
Others say it refers to real angels. However, the idea of a
human being in this context seems more satisfying.

Why? First, 'star' and 'messenger' are used in both the Old
Testament and New Testament to refer to humans. Next,
nowhere in the Bible are angels placed in a leadership position
over the church. Third, well established theology has concluded that Christ is not writing here to angels rather than
humans (2:1; 2:8; 2:12; 2:18; 3:1; 3:7; 3:14). Finally, humans
are responsible to God for the conduct of the church, not
angels (Hebrews 13:17).

The seven 'messengers' represent the human leadership of the church which is comprised of the elders/overseers. Paul outlines the requirements for such in 1 Timothy 3:1-7:

> It is a trustworthy statement: if any man aspires to the office of overseer, it is a fine work he desires to do. An overseer, then, must be above reproach, the husband of one wife, temperate, prudent, respectable, hospitable, able to teach, not addicted to wine or pugnacious, but gentle, uncontentious, free from the love of money. He must be one who manages his own household well, keeping his children under control with all dignity (but if a man does not know how to manage his own household, how will he take care of the church of God?); and not a new convert, lest he become conceited and fall into the condemnation incurred by the devil. And he must have a good reputation with those outside the church, so that he may not fall into reproach and the snare of the devil (for other details of their qualifications, see Acts 20:17, 28; Titus 1:5, 7; 1 Peter 5:1-5).

These messengers represent the leader of leaders for each assembly. That they are in Christ's right hand represents Christ's power over His churches. It reminds leaders that it is by Christ's authority they lead, not their own.

Letter outline

So it is that Christ, the Lord of the church, then writes seven letters to seven churches which are addressed to the ultimate leader of each church.

Although the letters follow a basic outline, the content of each letter differs. The letter to Ephesus illustrates the basic pattern:

1. Commission (2:1)
2. Commendation (2:2-3, 6)

3. Condemnation (2:4)
4. Confrontation (2:5)
5. Challenge (2:7)

Overcomers

Christ's promises to those who overcome form a common thread that runs through the challenge of these seven letters. They provide a bright spot, even in the dimmest letters written to Sardis and Laodicea.

An overcomer experiences victory over sin, Satan and the world. John already defined an overcomer in his first epistle: 'For whatever is born of God overcomes the world; and this is the victory that has overcome the world—our faith. And who is the one who overcomes the world, but he who believes that Jesus is the Son of God?' (1 John 5:4-5). As Christ overcame, so will those in Him also overcome and have the hope of eternal life in God's presence (Revelation 3:21).

At least fifteen magnificent promises are made to those who overcome*. They include eating from the tree of life (2:7), having power over the nations (2:26-27) and sitting with Christ at God's right hand (3:21).

The value of this study

Revelation expressly promises blessing for reading and obeying. 'Blessed is he who reads and those who hear the words of the prophecy, and heed the things which are written in it; for the time is near' (Revelation 1:3; 22:7). For this reason alone, every believer should master obedience to Revelation's demands so that God's blessing can be experienced.

Additionally, Revelation 2-3 commends to every Chris-

---

* You will find a summary listing of these fifteen promises on page 130.

tian what Christ finds delightful in the church. These are the qualities and activities that He desires to be cultivated in the church, whether we be in the pew or the pulpit.

Third, these seven letters warn against those things that Christ finds distasteful in His church. This section becomes Christ's pruning instructions for the Body (cf. John 15:1-2). Every true church of Christ needs to be cutting out those areas in the church which are displeasing to its Head.

To be more specific, at least ten broad implications for the church can be drawn in regard to Christ's mind about the church. In future chapters we will expand these general themes.

1. The church needs to continue in its first love and original deeds (Revelation 2:4-5).

2. The church must be prepared to suffer, if necessary, for Christ's sake (Revelation 2:9-10).

3. The church should maintain doctrinal integrity (Revelation 2:14).

4. The church needs to resolutely resist moral compromise (Revelation 2:20).

5. The church ought to remain useful to God (Revelation 3:16-17).

6. The church should continue on in ministry with uninterrupted steadfastness (Revelation 2:3, 2:13, 3:10).

7. The church must worship God alone (Revelation 22:9).

8. The church is mandated to obey God (Revelation 22:7).

9. The church ought to live holy (Revelation 2:2; 22:11).

10. The church exists to serve God (Revelation 2:2; 2:19; 22:12).

Christ made the ultimate sacrifice to establish the church, so we should render nothing less as we labour with the Lord of the church in continuing to build. We owe our best to the Master.

What does our best involve? Let me answer with an illustration. If we say that our best is 99.9%, and then go on to apply this standard of excellence in other areas of American life, it would result in two-million documents being lost by the Internal Revenue Service annually, 22,000 cheques being deducted from the wrong bank account each hour, 12 babies being given to the wrong parents each day, and 18,322 pieces of mail being mishandled every hour.

It's obvious that 99.9% is not good enough in the market-place. Therefore, only 100% will be acceptable to Christ as our best in the church.

2

EPHESUS
THE LOST LOVE CHURCH

To the angel of the church in Ephesus write: The One who holds the seven stars in His right hand, the One who walks among the seven golden lampstands, says this:

'I know your deeds and your toil and perseverance, and that you cannot endure evil men, and you put to the test those who call themselves apostles, and they are not, and you found them to be false; and you have perseverance and have endured for My name's sake, and have not grown weary.

'But I have this against you, that you have left your first love. Remember therefore from where you have fallen, and repent and do the deeds you did at first; or else I am coming to you, and will remove your lampstand out of its place— unless you repent. Yet this you do have, that you hate the deeds of the Nicolaitans, which I also hate.

'He who has an ear, let him hear what the Spirit says to the churches. To him who overcomes, I will grant to eat of the tree of life which is in the Paradise of God' (Revelation 2:1-7).

While the rest of Revelation focuses on the future, the first three chapters emphasize the things that have been and the things that are (1:19). They feature Christ and His bride—the church. The great promise of blessing for knowing and obeying in Revelation 1:3 refers primarily to what we do with the contents of chapters 1-3. Although we can do little today about the future recounted in chapters 4-22, we must share Christ's high priority for the church's purity and power outlined in the three chapters of Revelation 1-3.

Revelation 2-3 tells us what Christ thinks about His churches. We know that He loved the church enough to purchase her with His own blood (Acts 20:28), and that this commitment extended to building His church (Matthew 16:18). Caring enough to confront, Jesus now stands in the midst of the church to strengthen her. We find the mind of Christ for the church in these two significant chapters. In them we will discover what Christ commends and what He condemns in His church.

Christ started with Ephesus which existed before the other six. This church possessed prominence not known by Smyrna, Pergamum, Thyatira, Sardis, Philadelphia or Laodicea (1:11). Only the Ephesian church had been addressed previously in a New Testament letter written by an Apostle. On behalf of Christ, John now writes another piece of correspondence.

Commission (2:1)
Ephesus, modern day Seleuk in Turkey, shared supreme economic importance in the Middle East with Antioch and Alexandria. She existed as the gateway to Asia with a deep water port having access from the Aegean sea and served as the confluence for both north-south and east-west commercial land traffic.

Religiously, Ephesus housed the temple of Artemis, one of seven ancient wonders. This place of pagan worship measured 425 feet long by 220 feet wide and had 120 columns, each 60 feet high. Speaking of her moral climate, Heraclitus said no one could live in Ephesus without weeping at the immorality.

Founded in the second millennium BC, Ephesus had reached a population of over 150,000 by the time of Christ's letter. Geographically, Ephesus was the strategic city from which to evangelize Asia. Over 230 independent communities surrounded the city.

Christ, through Paul, placed a candlestick in this dark city when the Apostle ministered there longer than in any other locale (Acts 18-20). The church in Ephesus received many great Christians to trim her wick such as Aquila, Priscilla, Apollos, Paul, Silas, Timothy and John. Paul wrote an important New Testament letter to the Ephesian believers emphasizing the character and conduct of the church. Years later, he urged Timothy to remain on at Ephesus (1 Timothy 1:3). The church was well taught, with a 40-year tradition for faithfulness (ca. AD 55-95).

The letter is directed to the messenger of the church. In the previous chapter, I suggested that the *angelos* was human not angelic (1:20). The messenger can best be understood as 'the leader among leaders' in the church, or as representative of multiple, godly leadership. In either case, Christ writes to the highest responsible level of elder leadership.

Elder leadership derives its authority from God (Romans 13:1). However, this power has limitations that will be bounded by Scripture. One who has been called and empowered by God to lead the flock as a shepherd can lead with Divinely delegated authority for the purpose of leading the flock in the path of righteousness according to God's will as revealed in

Scripture. This undoubtedly is the sense of Hebrews 13:7, 'imitate their faith'. So Christ carries out His will in the church through elder leadership to the end that individual believers and the church corporately will be obedient to God's will in accordance with Scripture.

Christ introduces Himself as the one who holds the seven stars in His right hand, thus emphasizing His power through human leadership over the church. He also pictures His presence in the church as one who walks among the seven golden lampstands. The Ephesians needed to be reminded that this was Christ's church, not their own, and that He desired them to penetrate a spiritually dark city of worldwide prominence with the bright light of Christ's glory.

Commendation (2:2-3, 6)

Because Christ stood in their midst, He wrote, 'I know.' Jesus knew everything—both good and bad. He started with the positive by noting their service (2:2); comments are directed towards their performance (deeds), perspiration (toil) and perseverance (endurance). Ephesus modelled the working church as taught by Paul in Ephesians 4:11-12:

> And He gave some as apostles, and some as prophets, and some as evangelists, and some as pastors and teachers, for the equipping of the saints for the work of service, to the building up of the body of Christ.

Next he comments on their spiritual discernment (2:2,6). They had no room for evil men who, with their immorality, mocked Christ's Calvary sacrifice and God's holiness. Neither did they tolerate false apostles who could be objectively tested by comparing what they taught and how they lived to Scripture (Matthew 7:15-23; 2 Corinthians 11:13-15; 1 John

4:1-3). Paul's admonitions had prepared them:

> As a result, we are no longer to be children, tossed here and
> there by waves, and carried about by every wind of doctrine, by
> the trickery of men, by craftiness in deceitful scheming; but
> speaking the truth in love, we are to grow up in all aspects into
> Him, who is the head, even Christ (Ephesians 4:14-15).

Of particular significance was their shared hatred with
Christ for the Nicolaitans, a group of heretics who taught that
you could become a Christian and then continue living like the
rest of immoral Ephesus (2:6). Tradition often equated this
group's beginning with Nicolas of Antioch, mentioned in
Acts 6:5. Unbiblical licence had been sinfully confused with
Christian liberty.

Finally, Christ points to their staying power (2:3). He
compliments them for running to win (1 Corinthians 9:24)
with their eyes on Christ (Hebrews 12:1-2). They were a
'pressing on' type of church (Philippians 3:14). Needless to
say, we would be delighted to worship in such a church and
be even more amazed if Christ could find anything to criticize.
They were hard at work; they highly valued right living plus
pure doctrine; and they were not quitters. But, amazingly,
they were not the perfect church that they seemed to be. They
did not satisfy the Lord of the Church.

Condemnation (2:4-5)

Christ praised the Ephesians for who they were and what they
were doing. However, He also concerned Himself with what
they were not and what they were not doing, especially that
which had previously been their experience. They had left
their first love and had fallen from their first deeds.

At one time they had love for all the saints (Ephesians

1:15). Paul had prayed for them to know this love (Ephesians 3:17-19; 6:23). Now, several generations later, the love of the church had waned.

Note that while the letter is written to be read in the churches (2:7), it is specifically addressed to the leadership at Ephesus. Everywhere 'you' appears in the English version, it is in the second person singular in the Greek text. Jesus holds the God-appointed leadership responsible for communicating and correcting deficiencies in His church.

First Love (2:4)

The Ephesians had exchanged prominent love for peripheral love . What love had they left? What was different? What are we in danger of leaving? This love can be identified specifically by looking back to John's gospel and listening to Jesus' last instructions on love. He addresses three directions of love.

Christ begins with *upward love*. 'If you love Me, you will keep My commandments' (John 14:15, 21, 23). It's the love directed towards the Father and Son; it's the affection that actively seeks to deepen our relationship with God rather than the human tendency to become more involved with religion. Undoubtedly the Ephesians' worship, prayer and time in the Word suffered.

Next comes *inward love* or love of the brethren. 'Love one another, even as I have loved you ... By this shall all men will know that you are My disciples if you have love for one another' (John 13:34-35). A loss of this love focuses on church buildings and programs rather than on the more important 'body life' of the church. The ultimate of this love is sacrifice. 'Greater love has no one than this, that one lay down his life for his friends' (John 15:13). The Ephesians needed to re-emphasize this sacrificial love seen in serving one another.

Christ finally comments on *outward love*. 'As the Father has sent Me, I also send you' (John 20:21). The Father sent the Son with love for the world (John 3:16). As Christ sent the disciples so are we sent with the love of Christ to a loveless world. This lack of love is usually demonstrated by more desire to change society than to change the individuals who make up society through a personal relationship with the Lord Jesus Christ. Their hearts needed to be broken over the lostness and hell-bound future of a Christless world.

First Deeds (2:5)

Love is not an attitude alone. True love always demonstrates itself with action, 'And this is love, that we walk according to His commandments' (2 John 6); 'Let us not love with word or with tongue, but in deed and truth' (1 John 3:18). The Ephesians fell from their first deeds.

What were their deeds? Little is known about the church in its infancy, yet it probably was much like the early Jerusalem church (Acts 2-7). A careful study of 'the first church' tells us about its first deeds. In all likelihood these were the Ephesians' first deeds too.

1. They boldly penetrated their community with the gospel as an expression of outward love (Acts 2:1-42; 3:11-4:12).

2. They developed well-defined priorities to which they were highly committed as an expression of upward love (Acts 2:42).

3. They practised an uncommon preoccupation with one another's welfare as an expression of inward love (Acts 2:44-47; 4:32-35).

4. They possessed a supreme sense of God's holiness as an

expression of upward love (Acts 5:1-11).

5. They manifested the highest standards for spiritual leadership to which the congregation submitted as an expression of inward love (Acts 6:1-7).

6. They were willing to die for Christ's sake as an expression of outward love (Acts 7:54-60).

Confrontation (2:5)

Christ commended first before condemning. Now He confronts them with the consequences of their sin unless they change. The Lord of the church was not satisfied with a church that had a fruitful past or was currently better than most churches. He demanded a church that had no spot or wrinkle, being holy and blameless (Ephesians 5:25-27).

Jesus' pattern of confrontation is worth noting, as it models the process by which the leaders were to deal with the churches. Christians are to deal with other Christians in the same manner, as are parents with their children.

First, confronting was done with love and with the goal of restoration (2:4-5).

Second, encouragement preceded correction (2:2-3,6).

Third, Christ openly and concisely stated the problem (2:4-5).

Fourth, He told them how to be restored (2:5): remember your past, repent of your error, return to your best.

Fifth, Christ clearly laid out the consequences if they did not obey (2:5).

Sixth, He wrote with the expectation that they would respond positively (2:7).

So serious was Christ about the church's purity that He gave them an 'either ... or' option. In effect, He demanded that they either change and remain a light for Him; or He would come and remove the lampstand.

This has been God's patterned response to sin through the ages. For example, Israel as a nation was immobilized by Achan's sin (Joshua 7). God's Shekinah glory departed from the temple in the face of Judah's repeated spiritual harlotry (Ezekiel 8-11). Christ left His hometown of Nazareth with little witness of His miraculous power because they doubted Him (Matthew 13:53-58). God's *modus operandi* remains the same today in the church.

Jesus makes this point: the continued blessing of God on a given church is not guaranteed. Unless they continue in or return to 'first love attitudes' and 'first deed acts', they are in danger of Christ 'darkening' the life of the church.

Challenge (2:7)

The final words of this penetrating letter exhort 'the churches' to hear what God the Spirit is saying through God the Son. Often Christ and the Holy Spirit ministered closely in the church (cf. Romans 8:9 and Acts 16:6-7). These words are worth close attention. Christ writes in effect, 'Listen up! It will be applicable to all churches in all generations.' 'He who has an ear, let him hear ...' constitutes the Saviour's call to be doers of His word, not mere hearers alone (James 1:22). The Chief Shepherd will hold the flock accountable to obedience.

As in each of the seven letters, Christ concludes with promises for overcomers. 'Overcome' translates the Greek word *nikao* which describes a victorious soldier. Because our battle is against Satan, and because God has equipped us with spiritual armour (Ephesians 6:11, 13-20), believers in Jesus Christ are promised that they will overwhelmingly conquer through the Lord Jesus Christ (Romans 8:37).

To the victor is promised an eternal banquet from the 'tree

of life' in Paradise. That which was forbidden to the first Adam (Genesis 3:22) is promised to believers by Christ—the second Adam (cf. Romans 5:19). One who eats from this tree is one who lives for ever. It will be the main course in the New Jerusalem (Revelation 22:2, 14).

'Paradise' was used by the Persians of a park or garden; in the Septuagint (the Greek Old Testament), it is used of Eden (Genesis 2:8). The ancient Jews believed it was the place of blessing after death.

The New Testament uses 'Paradise' three times—each referring to the presence of God. It was Christ's promise to the crucified thief who believed (Luke 23:43) and the experience of Paul in the third heaven (2 Corinthians 12:4). Here, paralleling the previous two uses, it speaks of being in God's presence after death. Revelation 21-22 graphically describes the eternal experience of God's Paradise. Whatever price overcoming extracts in this life, the cost will be nothing compared to the incalculable benefits in eternity.

3

**SMYRNA
THE SUFFERING CHURCH**

And to the angel of the church in Smyrna write: The first and the last, who was dead, and has come to life, says this: 'I know your tribulation and your poverty (but you are rich), and the blasphemy by those who say they are Jews and are not, but are a synagogue of Satan.

'Do not fear what you are about to suffer. Behold, the devil is about to cast some of you into prison, that you may be tested, and you will have tribulation ten days. Be faithful until death, and I will give you the crown of life.

'He who has an ear, let him hear what the Spirit says to the churches. He who overcomes shall not be hurt by the second death' (Revelation 2:8-11).

Suffering has stalked the church since the beginning. Her Head suffered and died so that all who believe in Him might live (1 Peter 2:21-24). Those who initially followed Jesus rejoiced that they were counted worthy to suffer for His name (Acts 5:41). Paul testified: 'Now I rejoice in my sufferings for your sake, and in my flesh I do my share on behalf of His body (which is the church) in filling up that which is lacking in Christ's afflictions' (Colossians 1:24).

Of the original Apostles, all but one died a martyr's death. Even John, who died of natural causes, suffered for Christ's sake on the isle of Patmos. Early church tradition reports that Peter and Bartholomew were crucified upside-down, while Andrew died on an X-shaped cross. Matthew died by the sword in Ethiopia; Thomas was pierced with a lance; and Simon the Zealot was sawn in two. Both Matthias and Paul were beheaded, while Philip reportedly died by hanging.

Foxe's *Book of Martyrs* reports various kinds of punishments and cruelties imposed on early Christians.[1] These included imprisonment, racking, searing, boiling, burning, scourging, stoning and hanging. Many were lacerated with red hot pincers, and some were thrown upon the horns of wild bulls. Others were sewed up in the skins of wild beasts and then mauled by dogs; while still others were dressed in shirts made stiff with wax, fixed to trees and set on fire.

This kind of suffering by Christians continues to this day. As Smyrna was the first century 'suffering church', so the current suffering church has recently been found in places like China, Ethiopia, Zimbabwe and Albania. It has been reported that Christians in Russia were hung upside-down on ropes and beaten so severely that their bodies swung back and forth under the blows. Christians were put in 'refrigerator cells' which were so cold, frost and ice covered the inside.

The church at Smyrna needed a word of encouragement from the Lord of the church because of the intense persecution. So do we, for Paul advises that all who desire to live godly lives in Christ Jesus will be persecuted (2 Timothy 3:12). So Christ, through John, writes this second of seven letters to the churches of Asia. It serves especially to encourage those who suffer on account of their faithfulness to the Lord Jesus Christ.

Commission (2:8)

The angel, or better yet, 'messenger' of Smyrna represents the leadership of the church. The reasoning behind this interpretation has been fully developed in Chapter 1. Christ addresses His thoughts on the church of Smyrna to the spiritual leaders of the church.

Jesus taught, 'A pupil is not above his teacher; but everyone, after he has been fully trained, will be like his teacher' (Luke 6:40). The uniqueness of this church in Smyrna is a credit to courageous leadership and a compliment to the flock who willingly walked in the way of their elders.

> Obey your leaders, and submit to them; for they keep watch over your souls, as those who will give an account. Let them do this with joy and not with grief, for this would be unprofitable for you (Hebrews 13:17).

Smyrna, now modern Ismir in Turkey, is the only city among the seven which is still populated today. Located 35 miles north of Ephesus, Smyrna had no competition for splendour. Ancient coins described her as the 'first of Asia in beauty and size'.

Smyrna epitomized social sophistication. She boasted of her stadium, library and the largest public theatre in Asia. This noted city claimed to be the birthplace of Homer.

Pagan religion dominated the skyline. Mount Pagus rose 500 feet above the harbour and a famous thoroughfare called 'The Street of God' curved around her. Pagan shrines rested at both ends. One was devoted to Cybele or Sibylene Mother; the other to Zeus, chief god of the Greek pantheon. The acropolis on Mount Pagus was known as 'the crown of Smyrna'. Her population may have approached 200,000.

Smyrna existed as a self-sufficient city whose deities were thought to be the source of her success. Much as Christianity upset the economic balance in Ephesus (Acts 19:23-41), so the message of Christ's Lordship in Smyrna fostered violence against the church. Paganism did not mix economically with Christianity.

That is why Christ introduces Himself as 'the first and the last, who was dead, and has come to life.' He reminds the Christians there of His deity by pointing to His self-existent, eternal nature (Isaiah 41:4; 44:6; 48:12-16). They were suffering for the only true, living God. Their pain was not for a fraudulent cause nor in vain.

Then Christ turns to His humanity. He reminds them that He too suffered, even to death by crucifixion. But He won over death and rose again on the third day. Christ had experienced the worst that life could do to Him and then He conquered that which appeared at first to have the victory.

As Christ now writes to encourage, He writes in the strength of His deity, the apparent weakness of His death but the real power of His resurrection. Christ had been where the saints of Smyrna now are, and He made a way for them to be victorious, just as He had already been. Because death could not stop Christ, neither would it defeat the faithful at Smyrna.

Commendation (2:9)

Only two churches received commendation without condemnation—Smyrna and Philadelphia. Suffering produced a pure
and pleasing church to Christ. He commends the believers for
enduring tribulation, experiencing poverty and being subject
to blasphemy. How reassuring it must have been when the
church read, 'I know.'

Tribulation

Christ first comments on the pressure applied to the church.
It came from all sides. In all likelihood the most prominent
source was the government.

Smyrna served as a centre for emperor worship. In AD 23,
the city built the first temple in honour of Tiberius. Later on
in Domitian's rule (ca. AD 81-96), emperor worship was
imposed on every citizen with the threat of death for disobedience. Annually they had to burn incense on the altar of
Caesar. A certificate was then issued verifying the act.

That demand produced considerable pressure for Christians. To them Christ was Lord, not Caesar. While the
government requirement was more of a political loyalty than
a religious, yet to do so would compromise a Christian's
complete devotion to Christ. So they refused and were persecuted for faithfulness to Christ. They undoubtedly recalled
Christ's encounter with the Pharisees:

> Then the Pharisees went and counselled together how they
> might trap Him in what He said. And they sent their disciples
> to Him, along with the Herodians saying, 'Teacher, we know
> that You are truthful and teach the way of God in truth, and
> defer to no one; for You are not partial to any. Tell us therefore,
> what do You think? Is it lawful to give a poll-tax to Caesar or
> not?'

But Jesus perceived their malice, and said, 'Why are you
testing me, you hypocrites? Show Me the coin used for the poll-
tax.' And they brought Him a denarius. And He said to them,
'Whose likeness and inscription is this?'

They said to Him, 'Caesar's.'

Then He said to them, 'Then render to Caesar the things that
are Caesar's; and to God the things that are God's' (Matthew
22:15-21).

Poverty

As so often happened, Christianity had its economic implications. Undoubtedly it affected employment. Even if a person
were self-employed, it had an impact on the customers. Many
were disinherited by their family and were ostracized by the
community for their loyalty to Christ. These stand in contrast
with the church at Laodicea who said they were rich (3:17);
yet they were condemned by Christ. It's better to be poor and
commended, from Christ's perspective, than to be rich and
condemned.

Yet Christ told this church that they were rich, not in the
things of the world system like the Laodiceans who thought
they needed nothing, but rather in the things of God. That's
what James meant:

Listen, my beloved brethren: did not God choose the poor of
this world to be rich in faith and heirs of the kingdom which He
promised to those who love Him? (James 2:5).

Paul told Timothy to instruct the Ephesians to be rich in
good works (1 Timothy 6:18). He reminded the Corinthians
that although Christ was rich, yet for their sake He became
poor, so that through His poverty they could become rich (2
Corinthians 8:9). Paul taught the church at Rome that God
abounds in riches for all who call upon Him (Romans 10:12).

So Christ, who had less in this life than even the animals and birds (Matthew 8:20; Luke 9:58), refocused their attention on the eternal and spiritual. This reminder must have brought to their memory Christ's teaching:

> 'Lay up for yourselves treasures in heaven, where neither moth nor rust destroys, and where thieves do not break in or steal; for where your treasure is, there will your heart be also' (Matthew 6:20-21).

Blasphemy

In addition to pressure from the government and poverty imposed by the economic community, Christ also points to persecution from the religious establishment. As Revelation 2:9 comes to a close, Christ declares that those who say they are of God, but attack Christians, are really of Satan.

To blaspheme a Christian amounted to blaspheming Christ, just as persecuting a Christian was equivalent to persecuting Christ (Acts 9:4-5). In fact, the accusers of Christians in Smyrna would be accursed by God. They claimed to be Jews but were not. Like the Pharisees of Jesus' day, they were hypocrites and blind to God's truth (Matthew 23:1-39).

The problem for these people who claimed to be Jews occurred not in the physical lineage from Abraham but rather the spiritual (Galatians 3:7-9). That's why Paul wrote, 'For they are not all Israel who are descended from Israel' (Romans 9:6-7). Jeremiah further explains as he relays this message from God, 'I will punish all who are circumcised and yet uncircumcised' (Jeremiah 9:25). This is because they had never removed the foreskin of their heart (Deuteronomy 10:16; 30:6; Jeremiah 4:4).

A favourite expression of the Jews when they assembled was 'the assembly of the Lord' (Numbers 16:3; 20:4; 31:16).

Christ indicts the Jews who claimed to assemble on behalf of God but really gathered in the name of Satan. 'He who is not with me is against me' (Matthew 12:30). In similar fashion Christ told Peter, 'Get behind me Satan!' (Matthew 16:23).

What is the 'synagogue of Satan' (cf. Revelation 3:9)? This infamous title applies to any religious group who claims to gather in the name of the true God, but rejects Jesus Christ as the crucified and resurrected Saviour. To reject Christ is to accept Satan's lie and deceit.

There were six commonly reported slanders levelled against the early church by these so-called Jews.

1. Because Christians partook of Christ's body and blood, they were cannibals.

2. Because they called their common meal a love feast, Christians gathered for orgies of lust.

3. Because Christianity at times did split families, Christians were anti-family.

4. Because Christians worshipped without images, they were atheists.

5. Because Christians would not say, 'Caesar is Lord', they were politically disloyal.

6. Because they taught that the world ended with fire, Christians were incendiaries.

The Christians were obviously out of step with the city of Smyrna. Because they chose to walk with God, it seemed as if life were collapsing all around them. Undoubtedly, Christians there were asking, 'How should we react?' So Christ has some instructions for them on the subject of 'enduring'.

Challenge (2:10-11)

Christ gave a three-fold survival plan. It promised the bright hope of eternal life. Christ never promised to eliminate, or even alleviate pain in this life; but He did point them to a time when sin would be no more and righteousness would prevail.

Fear not

Step one is to trust God and not fear man. If anyone were to be feared it should be God (Luke 12:5). Yet there were some potentially fearful experiences for the church like the sufferings of prison, persecution and death.

Jesus alerts them for a second time that their battle is against the forces of Satan. This time He does not use the name Satan (adversary) but rather 'devil' (slanderer, cf. Revelation 12:10). Undoubtedly they would be imprisoned on false charges, whether political or religious, by so-called Jews who were unwittingly in league with Satan. The lion roared lies and the saints were devoured by imprisonment.

Notice that the incarceration was for 'testing'. It was the same kind of testing that Satan had imposed on Christ in Matthew 4:1-11. If these Christians of Smyrna were faithful to face the test with the sword of God's Word, as did Christ, they would emerge victorious as did Christ—even in death (James 1:2-4).

A 'ten day' prison sentence doesn't sound too rough at first glance, so interpreters have tried to make it more severe than it sounds. This has caused some to suggest that it refers to ten specific periods of Roman persecution. Others suggest that 'ten days' is a symbolic representation of a much longer period of time.

Personally I believe the 'ten days' should be taken at face value. It probably refers to a short imprisonment of ten days that ends in death. Regardless of whether it is ten days only or longer, Christ needed to exhort the Christians not to fear.

The words of Psalm 56:4 must have comforted them: 'In God I have put my trust; I shall not be afraid. What can mere man do to me?' They also would remember Jesus' Sermon on the Mount:

> 'Blessed are those who have been persecuted for the sake of righteousness, for theirs is the kingdom of heaven. Blessed are you when men cast insults at you, and persecute you, and say all kinds of evil against you falsely, on account of Me. Rejoice, and be glad, for your reward in heaven is great, for so they persecuted the prophets who were before you' (Matthew 5:10-12).

Be faithful

This was not a temporary assignment. For those who asked, 'How long?', Jesus answers, 'Until death!' As Christ was faithful unto death so are Christians to be also.

But the fight is not without a reward. It promises the crown of eternal life that celebrates victory over death (cf. James 1:12). In all likelihood, the crowns of the New Testament all refer to the reward of salvation that is received on the other side of death. Paul talks about the imperishable crown that celebrates victory over corruption (1 Corinthians 9:25) and the righteous crown that celebrates victory over unrighteousness (2 Timothy 4:8). Peter writes of the unfading crown of glory that celebrates the victory over that which is defiled and temporary (1 Peter 5:4).

Faithfulness will be rewarded, for God is a rewarder of those who seek Him (Hebrews 11:6). The believers in the church in Smyrna were not to back off of their faith because of hard times. Rather, they were to press on, move forward and keep looking up.

Listen carefully

Christ's last words to the church at Smyrna exhort them to listen carefully to what the Spirit says. It was an important message—'He who overcomes shall not be hurt by the second death.'

I have a friend who often wears a T-shirt with this message printed on it: 'Born twice, die once. Born once, die twice.' For one who is born again, the only death he or she will experience is physical. But one who is born only physically, that one will die twice—both physically and spiritually. For a Christian overcomer, the second death will not be experienced, therefore he will never know its conscious, eternal hurt.

In Rabbinic literature 'second death' referred to the death of the wicked in the next world. Biblically, the second death is equated with the lake of fire (Revelation 20:14). It is further described in Revelation 21:8:

> 'But for the cowardly and unbelieving and abominable and murderers and immoral persons and sorcerers and idolaters and all liars, their part will be in the lake that burns with fire and brimstone, which is the second death.'

The second death is equated with the conscious torment of eternal hell by those who have not received Christ as Saviour and Lord (cf. 2 Thessalonians 1:9).

For the Christian who shares in the first resurrection of which Christ is the first fruit (1 Corinthians 15:20), over this one the second death has no power (Revelation 20:6). The future prospect of the overcomer is to be a priest of God and Christ and reign with Christ for a thousand years.

A Striking Example

Because the letter ends here and nothing more biblically is written about Smyrna, we might wonder how the leadership responded to Christ's letter. Did they heed it or, later, because of fresh waves of pain and persecution, did they surrender to Satan? While not conclusive, we do have a historical hint at the answer to our question.

Polycarp would have been a young man when this letter was written and later read to the church. It must have had a profound effect upon him, for sixty years later he died a martyr's death as leader of the church of Smyrna. William Barclay reports the historical tradition surrounding Polycarp's death.

> So the crowds came flocking with faggots from the workshops and from the baths, and the Jews, even though they were breaking the Sabbath law by carrying such burdens, were foremost in bringing wood for the fire. They were going to bind him to the stake. 'Leave me as I am,' he said, 'for He who gives me power to endure the fire, will grant me to remain in the flames unmoved even without the security you will give by the nails.'
>
> So they left him loosely bound in the flames, and Polycarp prayed his great prayer: 'O Lord God Almighty, Father of Thy beloved and blessed Child, Jesus Christ, through whom we have received full knowledge of Thee, God of angels and powers, and of all creation, and of the whole family of the righteous, who live before Thee, I bless Thee that Thou hast granted unto me this day and this hour, that I may share among the number of the martyrs, in the cup of Thy Christ, for the resurrection to eternal life, both of soul and body in the immortality of the Holy Spirit. And may I today be received among them before Thee, as a rich and acceptable sacrifice, as Thou, the God without falsehood and of truth, hast prepared beforehand and shown forth and fulfilled. For this reason I also

praise Thee for all things. I bless Thee, I glorify Thee through the eternal and heavenly High Priest, Jesus Christ, Thy beloved Child, through whom be glory to Thee with Him and the Holy Spirit, both now and for the ages that are to come, Amen.'[2]

When on the verge of suffering, Christ prayed, 'My Father, if it is possible, let this cup pass from Me; yet not as I will, but as Thou wilt' (Matthew 26:39). Apparently, the church at Smyrna prayed in similar fashion.

4

PERGAMUM
THE COMPROMISING CHURCH

And to the angel of the church in Pergamum write: The One who has the sharp two-edged sword says this: 'I know where you dwell, where Satan's throne is; and you hold fast My name, and did not deny My faith, even in the days of Antipas, My witness, My faithful one, who was killed among you, where Satan dwells. But I have a few things against you, because you have there some who hold the teaching of Balaam, who kept teaching Balak to put a stumbling block before the sons of Israel, to eat things sacrificed to idols, and to commit acts of immorality. Thus you also have some who in the same way hold the teaching of the Nicolaitans. Repent therefore; or else I am coming to you quickly, and I will make war against them with the sword of My mouth. He who has an ear, let him hear what the Spirit says to the church. To him who overcomes, to him I will give some of the hidden manna, and I will give him a white stone, and a new name written on the stone which no one knows but he who receives it' (Revelation 2:12-17).

Revelation 2-3 provides the most comprehensive evaluation of the church in the New Testament. From Christ's analysis of the existing churches, we glean certain instructions on what to continue doing in the church and what to change.

We've already studied the 'lost-love' church at Ephesus and the 'suffering' church of Smyrna. Now we turn to the 'compromising' church in Pergamum. Like Ephesus, the Pergamum assembly is both commended and condemned.

Commission (2:12)

Sixty miles north of Smyrna and ten miles inland from the Aegean Sea lay Pergamum (modern day Bergama). The city rested on a hill one thousand feet in elevation. The ancient historian Pliny called Pergamum 'by far the most distinguished city in Asia'.

While not as commercially important like Ephesus and Smyrna, Pergamum made significant contributions. Politically, she served as the proconsular capital of Asia and the centre of emperor worship. A 200,000 volume library marked Pergamum as a chief centre of intellectual pursuit.

The great altar of Zeus (one of the seven ancient wonders) signified Pergamum's religious importance. This city was also the centre for worshipping Asklepios, the god of healing. In this respect, Pergamum served as a forerunner of modern day Lourdes.

Over the church in Pergamum, God's Holy Spirit had appointed overseers. To His 'messengers' Christ now writes an evaluation of their flock which undoubtedly encouraged them; but it also demanded that they exercise godly leadership to effect long overdue, righteous change as directed by the Chief Shepherd.

The letter unmistakeably points to these instructions as the very words of Christ. They are like a sharp, double-edged sword coming out of His mouth (cf. 1:16). His mouth represents the source and authority of this message from the Lord of the Church. The double-edged sword reminds us of the sword of the Spirit (Ephesians 6:17)—God's Word.

> For the word of God is living and active and sharper than any two-edged sword, and piercing as far as the division of soul and spirit, of both joints and marrow, and able to judge the thoughts and intentions of the heart (Hebrews 4:12).

Jesus threatens to come with this sword and wage war against His enemies in Pergamum; these are the Balaamites and the Nicolaitans (2:14-16).

Commendation (2:12-13)

To Ephesus Christ wrote, 'I know your deeds' (2:2), and to Smyrna, 'I know your affliction and your poverty' (2:9). 'I know where you live' is Christ's focus for those in Pergamum.

Christ knew that they lived in Satan's territory—that even his throne resided in their city. Satan reigns as 'the prince of this world' (John 12:31; 14:30; 16:11) and 'the god of this age' (2 Corinthians 4:4). Apparently, Pergamum served as a strategic hub of Satanic activity.

Satan's rule proved to be highly visible in Asia. Smyrna and Philadelphia housed synagogues of Satan, plus Thyatira hosted one of Satan's schools. In all likelihood, this mention of Satan's throne refers not to pagan idolatry, but rather to emperor worship whose Asian centre was Pergamum. The residents were constantly pressured by the imperial cult to worship a man (Caesar) rather than God. A secondary reference here could be to the idolatrous worship of Zeus and Asklepios.

In spite of all these temptations towards the counterfeit, the church had remained true to the name of Christ. They were steadfast in declaring 'Christ is Lord.' They had not succumbed to the secular religion of Caesar worship.

Neither did they renounce their faith in Jesus Christ. It was not to Asklepios that they looked as Saviour but rather to the only God and Saviour, Christ Jesus. They acknowledged Christ as Messiah and came to Him on His terms—faith alone. This continued even in the worst of times.

Apparently, the height of persecution existed in the days of Antipas, God's faithful witness who died for Christ's cause. Tradition tells us that Antipas had been summoned before the proconsul to sprinkle a few grains of incense on the fire and say 'Kurios Kaisar' or 'Caesar is Lord'. Refusing, he experienced the ultimate punishment; death by being slowly roasted to death in a brazen bull. This demonstrates why Christ called Satan a murderer (John 8:44).

Ever since, Antipas has been honoured as a martyr whose name and life have been handed down by God as a memorial to exemplify perseverance. To Antipas is accorded the description, 'My faithful witness', which is also ascribed to Christ (Revelation 1:5). They both died because of their faithful witness to the truth of God.

John and Betty Stam, modern day martyred missionaries to China, suffered the same kind of end as Antipas.

> As part of John and Betty's torture, the captors discussed whether they would kill the infant immediately to save trouble. But an unexpected protest arose from an onlooking Chinese farmer, who had been released from prison when communists sacked the town. He stepped forward to plead that the baby had done nothing worthy of death. 'Then it's your life for hers!' they retorted. 'I am willing,' he replied. He was chopped to pieces.

One man, a Christian doctor, fell to his knees and pleaded for the lives of his friends. He persisted until the Reds dragged him away to suffer death. Those who witnessed the approaching tragedy marvelled at the calmness with which John and Betty faced the worst their misguided enemies could do. John began to speak to the crowd, probably a Christian testimony, but the executioner cut his throat. Betty quivered. Still bound, she fell on her knees beside him. A quick command and the flash of a sword from behind reunited them for eternity.[1]

Condemnation (2:14-15)

Unfortunately, suffering had not perfected the church in Pergamum as it had the church in Smyrna, so the most striking word in our text is *but*. Although the believers had remained true to Christ under terrible adversity, compromise remained in the church—not in doctrine but rather in the Spirit generated dynamic of godly living.

Of Ephesus Jesus said, 'I have this against you' (2:4); but of Pergamum, Jesus noted, 'I have a few things against you,' summarised in the condemnation of two groups influenced by false teachers.

Balaamites (2:14)

First, there were those in the flock who held to the teachings of Balaam. Our text helps us to understand better this historical reference to Balaam in Numbers 22-25. On several occasions Balaam tried but failed in cursing Israel on King Balak's behalf.

Balaam struggled between being true to God's Word and his desire for honour among men. Even unbelieving King Balak diagnosed his problem, 'Therefore, flee to your place now. I said I would honour you greatly, but behold, the LORD has held you back from honour' (Numbers 24:11).

So badly did Balaam want the mammon of life that he finally succumbed to temptation. Although Balaam remained true to deliver God's message personally, he nevertheless instructed Balak on how to cause the Jews to bring a curse upon themselves. 'Behold, these caused the sons of Israel, through the counsel of Balaam, to trespass against the LORD in the matter of Peor, so the plague was among the congregation of the LORD' (Numbers 31:16). Consider the sad outcome:

> While Israel remained at Shittim, the people began to play the harlot with the daughters of Moab. For they invited the people to the sacrifices of their gods, and the people ate and bowed down to their gods. So Israel joined themselves to Baal of Peor, and the LORD was angry against Israel. And the LORD said to Moses, 'Take all the leaders of the people and execute them in broad daylight before the LORD, so that the fierce anger of the LORD may turn away from Israel.' So Moses said to the judges of Israel, 'Each of you slay his men who have joined themselves to Baal of Peor' (Numbers 25:1-5).

Men like Balaam existed in the first century, too. They rushed into Balaam's error for profit (Jude 10-11). These men only proved what Jesus said:

> No one can serve two masters; for either he will hate the one and love the other, or he will hold to one and despise the other. You cannot serve God and mammon (Matthew 6:24).

Peter rebuked and exposed the Balaamites in his writings:

> ... forsaking the right way they have gone astray, having followed the way of Balaam, the son of Beor, who loved the wages of unrighteousness, but he received a rebuke for his

own transgression; for a dumb donkey, speaking with the voice of a man, restrained the madness of the prophet (2 Peter 2:15-16).

In all likelihood there were those in the first-century church, parallel to Balaam, who told the Roman officials how to break down the Christian resistance to emperor worship. If the pattern held true, then they enticed them with immorality and the general lifestyle of idolaters.

The Balaamites preached God's Word in public, but in private they compromised the message like Balaam of old in their quest to be honoured by the world.

People like this exist today. Outwardly, like Balaam, they appear to speak for God and at times actually do. But inwardly, selfishness draws them away from God towards the fleeting honour and pleasure promised by the world. In so doing, they cause Christians to sin and bring God's chastisement on the church.

Nicolaitans (2:15)
On the other hand, the Nicolaitans also troubled the church. This group was not only local, for the Ephesian church also hated their practices, as did Christ (2:6).

Early church leaders such as Irenaeus and Hippolytus wrote that these were the followers of Nicolas, one of the seven men originally chosen to serve the Jerusalem congregation (Acts 6:5). It is probable that these false teachers reasoned that the human body was evil and that only the spirit was good. Therefore, a Christian could do whatever he wanted with the body and God's grace would be sufficient to cover fleshly sin.

This self-indulgent, libertine attitude contradicted all that Christ taught. Paul asks, 'Shall we go on sinning, so that grace may increase? By no means!' (Romans 6:1-2, NIV). Christ desires a radiant church, holy and blameless, without stain or wrinkle or any other blemish (Ephesians 5:27).

Both the Balaamites and the Nicolaitans were similar in that they seduced the church with idolatry and immorality. On the one hand, the Balaamites knew it was wrong but still sought after man's honour more than God's glory. On the other, the Nicolaitans tried to defend their unrighteous deeds as a lifestyle that did not contradict God's righteousness and holiness. In both cases, they corrupted the church and compromised their testimony for Christ.

Confrontation (2:16)

Compromise had invaded the church, so Jesus launched His counterattack. He tells them, 'Repent therefore!' In other words, turn away from the things of the world: ungodly worship and ungodly living. Embrace a holy passion for purity. Scripture teaches elsewhere, 'You adulteresses, do you not know that friendship with the world is hostility toward God? Therefore, whoever wishes to be a friend of the world makes himself an enemy of God' (James 4:4).

Christ lays out their two options—repent or else. At first glance, the consequence of disobedience does not sound too bad. 'I will soon come to you.' But then no one wants Christ to come and make war. A premature coming of Jesus spells trouble. His coming, with the sharp two-edged sword, would be to clean up the church. Just as He cleaned out the temple (Matthew 21:12-13), so He would purify His church.

Roman governors were divided into two classes, those who had the *ius gladii*, the right of the sword, and those who did not. Those who had the right also had the power of life and death.

The proconsul in Pergamum had the *ius gladii* humanly speaking and could use it at will against Christians. Here, Christ reminds them it would be better to experience the death sword of the Roman proconsul because they proved faithful to Christ rather than the sword of Christ who possessed the ultimate *ius gladii*.

Christ's sword is pictured as a battle sword of sizeable proportion. Here He uses this sword of His Word like a giant scalpel to excise the spiritual cancer of compromise out of the church.

Challenge (2:17)

As with all of His letters, Christ called on the churches to hear these important words. They are directed to the overcomers who can sing with Paul:

> But in all these things we overwhelmingly conquer through Him who loved us. For I am convinced that neither death, nor life, nor angels, nor principalities, nor things present, nor things to come, nor powers, nor height, nor depth, nor any other created thing, shall be able to separate us from the love of God, which is in Christ Jesus our Lord (Romans 8:37-39).

Their benediction rings out, 'But thanks be to God! He gives us the victory through our Lord Jesus Christ' (1 Corinthians 15:57).

Christ has already promised that the overcomer would eat of the tree of life (2:7), be given the crown of life (2:10), and be protected from the second death (2:11). Now, He adds two more magnificent promises.

First, the gift of hidden manna. God promised manna to the Jews in the wilderness (Exodus 16:15), but through Balaam's scheming, they compromised by eating food sacrificed to idols (Revelation 2:14). That kind of error is to be avoided by the church. Christ, the bread of life, is God's supply for eternal life (John 6:31-35). God's Word is our promise of food in this life to sustain our soul (Matthew 4:4). In eternity we shall be nourished from the tree of life (Revelation 22:2). 'Hidden manna' points to God's presently hidden provision for all of our needs in eternity to come.

Christ's next gift is intriguing. It will be a white stone with a new name written on it known only to the one who receives it. It is obviously unique to the individual overcomer. The stone most likely represents the redeemed person. The white colour pictures a person's righteousness in Jesus Christ. White seems to be heaven's colour as illustrated by white garments (Revelation 3:5), white robes (7:9), white linen (19:8,14) and God's white throne (20:11).

On that stone is written a new name. The Greek word translated 'new' means new in quality. It refers to the unique, new character of one belonging to heaven. We have been made new creatures by Christ (2 Corinthians 5:17) and in eternity all things will be made new (Revelation 21:5). The saints will live in the new Jerusalem (Revelation 3:12, 21:2) and sing a new song (Revelation 5:9).

Lessons For Today

The worldly, compromising church of the twentieth century can extract several implications from the compromising church of Pergamum for application today.

First, Christ knows our church situation—both the good and bad (2:13).

Next, He expects church leaders to do something constructive about that which Christ condemns (2:12).

Third, suffering for Christ is not enough. Until the church

is faithful and pure, Christ will not be satisfied (2:13-15). He demands purity.

Fourth, God's mercy prevails when we fail (2:16). This is the beauty and benefit of repentance.

Also, God's righteousness prevails when we disobey (2:16). That is the perfection of God's holiness which balances the tenderness of God's love.

Sixth, for those who run to the finish and fight to the end, there is great reward. Overcomers possess a glorious hope of hidden manna and a new name written down in glory (2:17).

5

THYATIRA
THE TOLERATING CHURCH

And to the angel of the church in Thyatira write:

The Son of God, who has eyes like a flame of fire, and His feet are like burnished bronze, says this: 'I know your deeds, and your love and faith and service and perseverance, and that your deeds of late are greater than at first.

'But I have this against you, that you tolerate the woman Jezebel, who calls herself a prophetess, and she teaches and leads my bond-servants astray, so that they commit acts of immorality and eat things sacrificed to idols. And I gave her time to repent; and she does not want to repent of her immorality. Behold, I will cast her upon a bed of sickness, and those who commit adultery with her into great tribulation, unless they repent of her deeds. And I will kill her children with pestilence; and all the churches will know that I am He who searches the minds and hearts; and I will give to each one of you according to your deeds. But I say to you, the rest who are in Thyatira, who do not hold this teaching, who have not known the deep things of Satan, as they call them—I place no other burden on you. Nevertheless what you have, hold fast until I come.

'And he who overcomes, and he who keeps My deeds until the end, to Him I will give authority over the nations; and He shall rule them with a rod of iron, as the vessels of the potter are broken to pieces, as I also have received authority from My Father; and I will give him the morning star. He who has an ear, let him hear what the Spirit says to the churches' (Revelation 2:18-29).

The longest of Christ's letters goes to the least significant, least known and least remarkable of the seven cities. Yet, the letter is extraordinary because no other church is quite so commended and condemned like Thyatira. Other than what we know from this letter, the history of this church is not recorded elsewhere.

Thyatira lay inland 40 miles southeast of Pergamum. Modern day Akhiser occupies the ancient site. Travelling clockwise in a circle from Ephesus, Thyatira is the fourth city one would visit.

Emperor worship did not dominate the religious society of Thyatira nor did major pagan deities. The local god, Tyrimnus, appeared on coins riding a horse and brandishing a battle-axe. Sambathe, a female prophetess, ruled the area's fortune-telling shrine.

Commercially, Thyatira differed from Ephesus, Sardis or Pergamum. This inland community could best be described as a 'blue collar' town. Trade guilds flourished in the fields of clothing, dying, tanning, making pottery, baking and bronze smithing. Thyatira served as Lydia's home where she dealt in purple cloth (Acts 16:14).

Commission (2:18)

As with previous letters, Jesus the Chief Shepherd writes to the leaders of the flock. Christ gives both extraordinary commendation and condemnation to these elders.

He wants them to know that these are not original words of John, even though John wrote them down. Rather, these thoughts come straight from 'The Son of God'. Only here in Revelation does Christ refer to Himself in such a way. He reminds them that He is true deity.

In light of idolatry in both the city and the church, Christ wanted there to be no mistake on this point.

Jesus zooms in on two of His personal features—His eyes and His feet. His eyes are like a blazing fire (cf. 1:14; Daniel 10:6). This symbolizes the all knowing and discerning mind of Christ. He knew everything, both good and bad. Nothing escaped His attention, not even sin. Just as the sins of Achan (Joshua 7) and Ananias and Sapphira (Acts 5) could not be hidden, neither could the sins of Jezebel in Thyatira.

Moving from head to toe, Christ next describes His feet as burnished bronze (cf. 1:15). Burnished bronze, a refined alloy of copper and metallic zinc, is both pure and strong. Christ pictures Himself as strong enough to conquer the church's enemies and pure enough to judge those who oppose him.

Christ purposely describes Himself as the all-knowing, true God who will defend the church by His might and judge her enemies righteously by His holiness. These qualities prove important when considering the major problems among this flock (cf. 2:23).

Commendation (2:19)
Christ finds two special qualities to compliment. Thyatira was a good church and it also was growing.

Five qualities in the church made it good: deeds, love, faith, service, and perseverance. Thyatira possessed everything that the Ephesian church had. Plus they had what Ephesus lacked: love and first deeds. Additionally, they practised the perseverance of Smyrna and exercised the faith of Pergamum. They also were growing in Christian maturity. They were doing more now than they did at first. The searching eyes of Jesus had carefully observed the best.

Condemnation (2:20)

'But I have this against you.' These dreaded words also pained the church at Ephesus and Pergamum. Christ knew all about the church and some of it He found unacceptable. Being a good, growing church did not minimize Christ's displeasure over their sin.

Christ's first charge was that the church tolerated the false prophetess Jezebel. Now, before we try to identify this wicked woman, a look at a little Old Testament background will help.

Jezebel is a unique name to the Bible. She was the daughter of Ethbaal, King of Sidon, and the wife of Ahab, King of Israel. She practised witchcraft (2 Kings 9:22), worshipped Baal and Asherah (1 Kings 16:32-33), supported hundreds of false prophets (1 Kings 18:19), and tried to eliminate the true prophets of God (1 Kings 18:4). She succeeded to the point that Elijah thought he was the only prophet left alive (1 Kings 18:22; 19:10).

In the incident with Naboth (1 Kings 21), Jezebel proved conclusively that she was a ruthless liar and a cold-blooded murderer. As a result of her God-scorned marriage to Ahab, she undermined his relationship with God.

There was never a man like Ahab, who sold himself to do evil in the eyes of the LORD, urged on by Jezebel his wife. He behaved in the vilest manner by going after idols, like the Amorites the LORD drove out before Israel (1 Kings 21:25-26, NIV).

With that in mind, look at the Jezebel of Thyatira. She was a false prophetess who had not been commissioned by God, unlike Miriam (Exodus 15:20), Deborah (Judges 4:4), Huldah (2 Kings 22:14) or the four daughters of Philip (Acts 21:9).

She misled and deceived Christ's servants rather than directing them on the path of truth.

Jezebel joins a long list of Christ's infamous enemies. There were those who preached another gospel (Galatians 1:6-10) and those who legalistically tried to revert back to the Mosaic law (Colossians 2:8, 16-19). Hymaneus and Philetus taught false doctrine (2 Timothy 2:16-18), as did the false prophets whom Peter (2 Peter 2:1-3), John (1 John 4:1-3) and Jude (Jude 4) condemned.

The authenticating mark of a true prophet is that his or her words agree with God's Word. Jezebel's did not.

> But a prophet who presumes to speak in my name anything I have not commanded him to say, or a prophet who speaks in the name of other gods, must be put to death.
>
> You may say to yourselves, 'How can we know when a message has not been spoken by the LORD?' If what a prophet proclaims in the name of the LORD does not take place or come true, that is the message the LORD has not spoken. That prophet has spoken presumptuously. Do not be afraid of him (Deuteronomy 18:20-22, NIV).

Jezebel condoned sexual immorality and eating food sacrificed to idols. Both Testaments speak against these sinful practices:

> You must not live according to these customs of the nations I am going to drive out before you. Because they did all these things, I abhorred them (Leviticus 20:23, NIV).

> If a man commits adultery with another man's wife—with the wife of his neighbour—both the adulterer and the adulteress must be put to death (Leviticus 20:10, NIV).

> Instead we should write to them, telling them to abstain from
> food polluted by idols, from sexual immorality, from the
> meat of strangled animals and from blood .... You are to
> abstain from food sacrificed to idols, from blood, from the
> meat of strangled animals and from sexual immorality. You
> will do well to avoid these things (Acts 15:20, 29, NIV).

Christ refers to these sins as 'Satan's so called deep secrets'
(2:24). It could be that they actually called their teachings 'the
deep things of God' and Christ is emphatically setting the
record straight. Or it could be the beginnings of later Gnostic
thought that reasoned, in order to defeat Satan and gain an
appreciation for God's grace, one had to enter Satan's strong-
hold and experience the darkness of sin.

In either case, God judged Jezebel's teachings as abomina-
ble. The Bible soundly condemns those who teach that evil
deeds are righteous: 'Woe to those who call evil good, and
good evil; who substitute darkness for light and light for
darkness; who substitute bitter for sweet and sweet for bitter!'
(Isaiah 5:20).

How could this happen in such a highly commended
church (cf. 2:19)? Remember that Thyatira was a commercial
centre noted for its trade guilds. These guilds were married to
false religion. They each had their own patron deity to whom
they paid homage in exchange for supposed economic blessing. These pagan practices would have involved a combination of idolatry and immorality.

After becoming a Christian, there could be no more idolatry or immorality because 'Jesus is Lord'. No more sinful
worship meant no more trade guild membership. This resulted in severe personal economic problems.

Apparently, a Jezebel-like lady in the church taught that

you could continue practising pagan rites in the trade guilds, yet still find favour with God in the church. Exactly who she was remains unknown although some have tried to identify her with Lydia or the pastor's wife. Double trouble existed because she not only taught false doctrine, but the leaders of the church tolerated it. They allowed her to teach and lead Christ's bondservants astray.

So Christ condemns them all soundly. The church is to be pure both doctrinally and practically. Unity at the expense of purity is false unity. Paul reminded the Corinthian church to 'flee immorality' and to 'flee from idolatry' (1 Corinthians 6:15-20; 10:14).

Confrontation (2:20-23)

Christ targeted four major groups in his stinging rebuke:

> (1) the church leaders,
> (2) Jezebel,
> (3) her spiritual consorts and
> (4) their offspring.

Church leaders (2:20)

'I have this against you.' The elders tolerated, or literally in Greek 'forgave', an unrepentant person. Apparently they confronted Jezebel, and when she appeared to repent, they trusted her then as a forgiven person.

However, she had not actually repented. As evidence to support this assertion, Christ reminds them that she continued to mislead. Nothing mocks God's mercy and grace more than to reject God's forgiveness and then to be treated as a repentant person. The elders should have known better and acted differently.

Jezebel (2:21-22a)

It was not that God did not want her to repent. He gave her time but she chose to reject God's offer. Jezebel exerted her own will to the exclusion of God's will.

This is not without consequence. God will cast her on a bed of suffering. It would not be the first time God rebuked a rebellious person this way. Lot's wife (Genesis 19), Korah (Numbers 16), Aaron (Numbers 20), Moses (Deuteronomy 34), Gehazi (2 Kings 5), Ananias and Sapphira (Acts 5), Herod Agrippa (Acts 12) and the Corinthians (1 Corinthians 11) all experienced physical suffering handed out by God. The Son of God has the power both to give life and to withdraw it.

Fellow adulterers (2:22b)

Those who shared the bed of spiritual harlotry with Jezebel also would suffer. God promised great tribulation unless they too repented as He demanded. If no-one had been willing to join her, Jezebel's cause would have failed. However, some joined her in giving birth to another generation.

Jezebel's offspring (2:23a)

Christ goes one step further. He promised the first generation suffering and tribulation, but to those in the second he threatens now with death.

Why be so brutal to those who were duped by Jezebel? Because second generation heretics are more dangerous in that they quickly produce a third-generation. With this, they will have spawned a seemingly unstoppable movement. Jesus spoke similarly to the Pharisees, 'Woe to you, teachers of the law and Pharisees, you hypocrites! You travel over land and sea to win a single convert, and when he becomes one, you make him twice as much a son of hell as you are' (Matthew 23:15).

While there was the promise of economic prosperity as a result of false teaching, it actually ended in spiritual bankruptcy for those who followed Jezebel. Sin, regardless of the apparent reward, is not to be tolerated in the church.

Just in case other churches reading this letter to Thyatira might become smug, Jesus adds a note for them (2:23b). Christ knows all about the other churches too and will judge them for reward or retribution according to their deeds, just like He did in the case of Jezebel and Thyatira. Christ's eyes, like a flame of fire, miss nothing.

The church at Thyatira needed to adopt this prayer.

Search me, O God, and know my heart;
Try me and know my anxious thoughts;
And see if there be any hurtful way in me,
And lead me in the everlasting way (Psalm 139:23, 24).

Paul gives us some insight into what Jesus meant: 'For we must all appear before the judgment seat of Christ, that each one may be recompensed for his deeds in the body, according to what he has done, whether good or bad' (2 Corinthians 5:10). Every believer must appear at God's *bema* or judgment seat. There will be spiritual consequences for our sins as true believers.

Challenge (2:24-29)

There is actually a fifth group, but they are not confronted with sin, rather challenged to stay pure. They are 'the rest in Thyatira' who have separated themselves from Jezebel and her teaching.

These must hold fast to the truth that they have, and never

grab for that which pollutes. They were to do this until Jesus comes for them. They were also to persevere in the truth of God's Son, the Lord Jesus Christ.

Apparently, other than on this one major issue, the Thyatira church was clean. Jesus promised not to place any other burden on them (2:24).

When Jesus does come He will reward those who overcome. Overcomers are further defined here as those who do Christ's will to the end, which is marked out by Christ's arrival (2:25-26). They are the ones who believe that Jesus is the Son of God. Their profession of faith is lived out in their pursuit of life.

For those who will to do God's will, unlike Jezebel who along with her consorts and their children were unwilling, God wills to reward with authority over the nations (2:26). This thought is not new to Scripture.

'And I confer on you a kingdom, just as my Father conferred one on me, so that you may eat and drink at my table in my kingdom and sit on thrones, judging the twelve tribes of Israel' (Luke 22:29-30, NIV).

Do you not know that the saints will judge the world? And if you are to judge the world, are you not competent to judge trivial cases? (1 Corinthians 6:2, NIV).

You have made them to be a kingdom and priests to serve our God, and they will reign on the earth (Revelation 5:10, NIV).

I saw thrones on which were seated those who had been given authority to judge. And I saw the souls of those who had been beheaded because of their testimony for Jesus and because of the word of God. They had not worshipped the beast or his image and had not received his mark on their foreheads or their hands. They came to life and reigned with Christ for a thousand years. Blessed and holy are those who have a part in the first resurrection. The second death has no power over them, but they will be priests of God and of Christ and will reign with him for a thousand years (Revelation 20:4-6, NIV).

Psalm 2:7 quoted in Revelation 2:27 might seem strange at first. Jesus reminds those who would question His right to give His authority to His followers that it was given to Him by His Father as stated in Psalm 2. Thus, He had every right to give it to whoever He chooses.

Jesus' point is this—the one who proves faithful in the little things of this life will be entrusted with greater responsibilities in the kingdom to follow.

A second reward promised is 'the morning star' (2:28). This phrase is found only in one other place in the New Testament: 'I, Jesus, have sent my angel to testify to you these things for the churches. I am the root and the offspring of David, the bright morning star' (Revelation 22:16). Jesus is that star who promises to give Himself to His faithful followers. For without Him to rule as King of Kings and Lord of Lords (Revelation 19:16), our authority would be hollow and without glory.

As a final note, Christ closes in His usual fashion with a reminder that all churches can learn from the lessons in this letter (2:29). 'Churches' includes all churches then and now. These conclusions can be gleaned from His instructions.

1. It is not enough to hear only and then do nothing about it.

2. It is not enough to hear and then do anything you want to do, like Jezebel.

3. Even if elders in the church tolerate sin, Christ will never do so because He died in order to receive a pure bride.

4. The only thing that pleases Christ is total obedience, like that demonstrated by 'the rest of you in Thyatira'.

Jesus' letter to Thyatira is best summarized by remembering His striking words in Matthew:

Therefore everyone who hears these words of mine and puts them into practice is like a wise man who built his house on the rock. The rain came down, the streams rose, and the winds blew and beat against that house; yet it did not fall, because it had its foundation on the rock. But everyone who hears these words of mine and does not put them into practice is like a foolish man who built his house on sand. The rain came down, the streams rose, and the winds blew and beat against that house, and it fell with a great crash (7:24-27, NIV).

It did not matter that the church in Thyatira was good and growing. If the elders did not deal with Jezebel and her spiritual harlotries, the church would eventually fall with a great crash. The Chief Shepherd refused to tolerate false doctrine and ungodly living. He loved the church too much to let the believers return to the sin from which they had been saved.

6

**SARDIS
THE DYING CHURCH**

And to the angel of the church in Sardis write:

He who has the seven Spirits of God, and the seven stars, says this: 'I know your deeds, that you have a name that you are alive, but you are dead. Wake up, and strengthen the things that remain, which were about to die; for I have not found your deeds completed in the sight of My God. Remember therefore what you have received and heard; and keep it, and repent. If therefore you will not wake up, I will come like a thief, and you will not know at what hour I will come upon you.

'But you have a few people in Sardis who have not soiled their garments; and they will walk with Me in white; for they are worthy. He who overcomes shall thus be clothed in white garments; and I will not erase his name from the book of life, and I will confess his name before My Father and before His angels. He who has an ear, let him hear what the Spirit says to the churches' (Revelation 3:1-6).

Christ desires to present the church to Himself in all her glory without stain or wrinkle—a holy and blameless church (Ephesians 5:27). The holy character of the church lives out God's redemptive purpose in personal salvation because He chose her in Him to be holy and blameless in His sight (Ephesians 1:4).

Somehow the church at Sardis had missed this point; their brand of Christianity had made peace with its pagan environment. Sardis became the perfect model of inoffensive Christianity, adding nothing righteous to change the bitter taste of sin in society. The church's light was so dim that it did not even disturb the darkness which enshrouded the city.

The church desperately needed revival. While the believers in Ephesus had left their first love, the Sardians were in danger of losing their life. Here, Christ mandates a major course correction to comply with His order in Matthew 5:16: 'Let your light shine before men in such a way that they may see your good works and glorify your Father who is in heaven.'

If churches could be admitted to hospital, the body at Sardis would unquestionably be taken to the Intensive Care Unit. We stand warned by her sad example that alive, vibrant churches can become diseased and decline in spiritual health to the danger point of dying.

Commission (3:1a)

As discussed previously, 'the angel' represents the church's leadership. They shouldered Christ's commission to watch over the flock for which they must one day give an account to the Chief Shepherd (Hebrews 13:17). As Christ's undershepherds, they served as God's human overseers for the church in Sardis.

Sardis lay 35 miles southeast of Thyatira and 50 miles east

of Smyrna. She was one city in two locations. One location was atop Mount Tmolus, 1,500 feet in elevation, the other at the foot of Mount Tmolus in the Hermus River valley.

Three separate spiritual strands comprised the major chord of religious emphasis in Sardis. As in most cities the Caesar cult or Emperor worship flourished. Akin to Ephesus, Sardis also housed a major temple devoted to the worship of Artemis (Diana). The worship of Cybelle, a local nature goddess, paralleled similar idolatrous practices in Smyrna.

The city's secular past was far more distinguished than the time when John wrote. She had been unable to sustain and repeat her past glories. Unfortunately, the church in Sardis walked in the city's footsteps rather than Christ's.

Christ introduced Himself as the one who has the seven spirits of God and the seven stars. Using the imagery of Zechariah 4 which equates a seven lamp lampstand with God's Spirit, the 'the seven spirits of God' in Revelation 1:4 also refers to the Holy Spirit. Revelation 4:5 also pictures the seven spirits as seven lamps of fire, while Revelation 5:6 equates them with seven eyes. 'Seven' is used here in a figurative sense of perfection fitting the deity of the Holy Spirit.

Earlier, 'the seven stars' were identified as the perfection of leadership in the church (Revelation 1:16, 20) which Christ holds in His right hand of authority. These represent the current leadership in the church which Christ holds accountable for the prevailing conditions. Christ's focus seems to be on the leadership gap at Sardis. There must have been a woeful lack of Spirit-controlled human leadership. Only a shortfall of Spirit power could account for what Christ is about to say. The church's leadership undoubtedly ignored or minimized the ministry of God's Spirit who:

•gives life—Romans 8:9

•lives in believers—1 Corinthians 6:19

•leads believers—Romans 8:14

•produces spiritual fruit—Galatians 5:22-25

•gives gifts—1 Corinthians 12:11

•promotes unity—Ephesians 4:3

All of the necessary ingredients for a dynamic, vibrant church are available to church leadership. Where there is a lack of power and life in the church, there is a lack of receiving from the Lord Jesus Christ and the Holy Spirit. Christ writes in effect, 'There is no excuse for your pitiful state, so I now write to condemn the church with the hope that you will recover.'

Condemnation (3:1b)
In the previous letters, the phrase 'I know your deeds' has been used at the beginning of commendation: Ephesus (2:2), Smyrna (2:9), Pergamum (2:13), and Thyatira (2:19).

But there is no commendation here, only condemnation. This will be the first of two letters in which Christ has nothing good to say about the church. In the other cities, evil proved to be an exception; in Sardis evil ruled. Only one other church had the notoriety of having nothing good said about it—Laodicea.

The church possessed a 'reputation of being alive', but Christ comments, 'You are dead.' Society had put its stamp of approval on Sardis, but God was about to write Ichabod (1 Samuel 4:21) or 'no glory'. Jesus had warned others of this earlier, 'Woe to you when all men speak well of you, for in the same way their fathers used to treat the false prophets' (Luke 6:26).

The Sardian church stood as a double contradiction. First, what the world said they were, they were not—to their own shame. Then, what God designed them to be, they were not—also to their own shame.

Christ intended the church in Sardis to be alive, not dead. The church of Christ is made up of living stones (1 Peter 2:4-5), in each of whom dwells the living God (2 Corinthians 6:16). Their source of life is the Lord Jesus Christ (Galatians 2:19-20).

Sardis stands in contrast to the 'suffering church' of Smyrna. Sardis thought she was alive because she was so acclaimed by the community, but God diagnosed her as dying. On the other hand, the residents of Smyrna sought to eliminate the church through physical death, but God promised her the crown of life (Revelation 2:10).

What elements of life did the 'dying church' at Sardis lack? A biblically alive church like Smyrna certainly was marked by these 'vital signs'. In contrast, Sardis would have been just the opposite.

• Love for and submission to God's Word (1 Peter 2:1-3).

• Desire for God's approval (2 Corinthians 5:9).

• Quest for holiness (1 Peter 1:14-16).

• Servant attitude (Romans 12:10-13).

- Proclamation of the gospel (Luke 24:47).

- Discipleship of believers (Matthew 28:19-20).

- Emphasis on strong spiritual leadership (1 Timothy 3:1-13).

- Sending out reproducers to other locations (Acts 13:1-3).

- Regularity in prayer (1 Thessalonians 5:17).

- Growth in quality and quantity (2 Peter 3:18; Acts 2:47).

- Unwillingness to compromise (Ephesians 6:11).

Whatever the Sardian church did, she was not focused on these major objectives. The church proved hollow to Christ—hypocritical and outwardly deceptive. Like a white-washed tomb or desert mirage, the church promised much but delivered very little, if anything.

Confrontation (3:2-3)
The message to Sardis was 'Be cured or else you'll die.' Note that Christ did not say, 'You are dying and I have come to bury you.' Rather, He openly confronted the church with the reality of impending death if nothing was done to reverse their course. Then He outlined a five point recovery process for them. The rest was then up to the church.

Step One
First, 'Wake up!' Christ calls the believers to come out of their stupor. Whatever they had been on or whatever they were preoccupied with that caused spiritual dullness, they needed

to abandon it instantly. They had to acknowledge the problem and get away from their source of death. Before they could solve the problem, they had to admit they were out of order and take this first step to get back in line with the truth.

Step Two
Next comes spiritual rehabilitation. Christ orders them to 'strengthen what remains and is about to die'. This same thought occupied Paul's heart for other churches. He writes to Rome, 'I long to see you in order that I may impart to you some spiritual gift to you to make you strong' (Romans 1:11). Paul sent Timothy to the Thessalonians to strengthen and encourage them in their faith (1 Thessalonians 3:2).

Christ gave the believers in Sardis a warning. Unless they could come back and regain their former health, God's purpose in their lives would not be fulfilled (Ephesians 2:10). They would be like the foolish man who laboured long and hard, but in the end his home lay destroyed because he did not follow the Lord's instructions (Matthew 7:24-27).

Step Three
'Remember what you have received and heard' follows. Peter once wrote to remind the dispersed church of what he previously had taught (2 Peter 1:12-15); now Christ also calls the dying church to remembrance. Like the Thessalonians who had received Paul's teaching as the Word of God (1 Thessalonians 2:13), so the Sardis believers needed to return to the Word first preached to them.

They evidently had fallen into the same trap as the Galatians, who had departed from what they had first been taught (Galatians 3:1-5). So, they were to return to God's Word which is sharper and quicker than any two-edged sword

(Hebrews 4:12), and which would be profitable for teaching, rebuking, correction and training in righteousness to the end that they would be thoroughly equipped for every good work (2 Timothy 3:16-17).

Step Four
Now they needed to 'obey it'. Knowledge of the Word alone will never bring life—only the keeping of it promotes life. This assembly needed to learn from the Philadelphian church of whom Christ says, 'You have kept My word' (Revelation 3:8).

Step Five
Finally, Christ commands them to 'repent'. They needed to alter their current course in order to walk with God. The leadership had to acknowledge their sin and turn away from it. In so doing, they were to get in step with the Lord of the church and lead the church on the pathway of righteousness.

That raises an important question: What if they chose to disregard Christ's warning? Knowing the deceitful heart of even Christian leaders, Jesus gave this ultimatum, 'If therefore you will not wake up, I will come like a thief, and you will not know at what hour I will come upon you.'

Christ had already told the Ephesians to change or He would remove their lampstand (2:5). Pergamum was warned to change their ways or Christ would come to fight (2:16). This promised coming to Sardis would certainly not be joyful and pleasant but terribly sad. But none of these warnings would not materialise if only the Sardis church would submit to Christ and the Holy Spirit.

All this makes us wonder how a true church could ever reach this low estate. However, all of the verbs used here in

Christ's orders to Sardis (wake up, strengthen, remember, keep, repent) have, in the past, addressed the true church and therefore probably do so here also.

The church of Christ has been commanded to:

- Pray in the Spirit (Jude 20)

- Preach in the Spirit (1 Thessalonians 1:5)

- Worship in the Spirit (John 4:24)

- Live in the Spirit (Galatians 5:25)

- Walk in the Spirit (Galatians 5:16,25)

However, the church can grieve the Spirit with sin (Ephesians 4:30) and quench the Spirit with wilful disobedience (1 Thessalonians 5:19). That is undoubtedly what happened at Sardis, which serves as the classic example of the 'self-willed' rather than the 'Spirit led' church. Just as individual believers can resist the Spirit, so can entire churches. Also, there were probably many counterfeit Christians in the church at Sardis.

Challenge (3:4-6)

There is good news for those who are more concerned with pleasing God than man. In Sardis, a few people had not yet 'soiled their garments'. Even under the worst of conditions these saints should have comprised the majority, but sadly Christ reported that they were a small minority.

The fact that they had not soiled their garments cannot mean they had not sinned after salvation (1 John 1:8-10). But rather these with clean clothing are the faithful remnant of true believers who confessed and repented of sin in their Christian life on a regular basis (1 John 1:9).

These are the kind of people Christ desires to accompany Him who will be dressed in white—the colour of heaven. Their robes are white because they have been washed in the blood of the lamb (Revelation 7:13-14). White robes represent a believer's salvation in Jesus Christ. Isaiah and Paul vividly portray this forgiveness of sin.

'Come now, and let us reason together,'
Says the LORD,
'Though your sins are as scarlet,
They will be as white as snow;
Though they are red like crimson,
They will be like wool' (Isaiah 1:18).

What is more, I consider everything a loss compared to the surpassing greatness of knowing Christ Jesus my Lord, for whose sake I have lost all things. I consider them rubbish, that I may gain Christ and be found in Him, not having a righteousness of my own that comes from the law, but that which is through faith in Christ—the righteousness that comes from God and is by faith (Philippians 3:8-9, NIV).

Thus, they are worthy not in themselves, but rather in Christ.

These believers also have Christ's authentication because their names are written in the book of life from which they cannot be erased. This book is mentioned six times in Revelation (3:5; 13:8; 17:8; 20:12; 20:15; 21:27). It is variously called 'the book of life', 'the book of life belonging to the Lamb' and 'the Lamb's book of life'.

Most likely in this one book are recorded the names of

everyone who has ever lived. Those who are spiritually alive in Christ and will never die (John 11:25-26) remain in the book; as overcomers their names will never be erased. Conversely, those who physically die outside of Christ will be spiritually dead for eternity (2 Thessalonians 1:9) and thus their names are erased at death. Just as was the practice in the citizen registry of an earthly city, so it will be in heaven.

Overcomers will also have Christ's acknowledgement before the Father and the angels. Here Christ reaffirms what He taught while on earth:

> 'Whoever acknowledges me before men, I will also acknowledge Him before My Father in heaven. But whoever disowns Me before men, I will disown him before My Father in heaven' (Matthew 10:32-33, NIV).

> 'I tell you, whoever acknowledges Me before men, the Son of Man will also acknowledge him before the angels of God. But he who disowns me before men will be disowned before the angels of God' (Luke 12:8-9, NIV).

The believer's heavenly Advocate is Jesus Christ (1 John 2:1).

One final note concluded Christ's letter to Sardis. 'He who has an ear, let him hear what the Spirit says to the churches.' All other churches stand warned to avoid the error of the Sardis church—that of ignoring God's Spirit. To do so could lead to a dying church and Christ's premature arrival in judgment.

Lessons to learn
The admonition of Revelation 3:6 applies to contemporary churches as well as to the churches of John's day. Take careful

note of these applications and then, where needed, apply them to your church.

1. Don't take too seriously what outside people say about your church.

2. Look to God and His Word for an evaluation of how well you are doing rather than to some unbiblical standard.

3. Regularly remind yourself about the constant danger of complacency and compromise.

4. Don't reject divine leadership by God's Spirit or the human leadership of elders led by God's Spirit.

5. When you find areas of spiritual deadness, apply Jesus' five step recovery process.

6. Take courage in Jesus' promise of eternal reward for those who overcome.

John Wesley captured Christ's desire for committed leadership and followership in the church with these striking words:

> Give me one hundred preachers who fear nothing but sin and desire nothing but God, and I care not a straw whether they be clergy or laity, such alone will shake the gates of hell, and set up the kingdom of God on earth.

7

PHILADELPHIA
THE OBEDIENT CHURCH

And to the angel of the church in Philadelphia write: He who is holy, who is true, who has the key of David, who opens and no one will shut, and who shuts and no one opens, says this: 'I know your deeds. Behold, I have put before you an open door which no one can shut, because you have a little power, and have kept My word, and have not denied My name. Behold, I will cause those of the synagogue of Satan, who say that they are Jews, and are not, but lie—behold, I will make them to come and bow down at your feet, and to know that I have loved you. Because you have kept the word of My perseverance, I also will keep you from the hour of testing, that hour which is about to come upon the whole world, to test those who dwell upon the earth.

'I am coming quickly; hold fast what you have, in order that no one take your crown. He who overcomes, I will make him a pillar in the temple of My God, and he will not go out from it anymore; and I will write upon Him the name of My God, and the name of the city of My God, the new Jerusalem, which comes down out of heaven from My God, and My new name. He who has an ear, let him hear what the Spirit says to the churches' (Revelation 3:7-13).

John in his gospel has already recorded Christ's earlier declaration: 'Whoever has my commands and obeys them, he is the one who loves me' (John 14:21, NIV). In his letter to the church in Philadelphia, Christ explains how this fleshes out in the life of the church.

Philadelphia existed as a rose between two thorns—Sardis the 'dying' church and Laodicea the 'useless' church. Christ has only condemnation for those two churches, but for Philadelphia the Chief Shepherd has nothing but praise for obedience. Where the Ephesian church failed, the Philadelphian church excelled.

The letter courier would have journeyed about 30 miles southeast of Sardis to Philadelphia, the youngest of the seven cities. The city of brotherly love was originally founded to be a mission point of Greek culture and language to Lydia and Phrygia. Philadelphia stood at the border of these countries; and because of a major thoroughfare going through Philadelphia, it served as the commercial gateway from Europe to the east. Now Christ strategically uses Philadelphia as a centre to spread the gospel into adjacent regions. Philadelphia would serve God's higher missionary purposes.

Commission (3:7)
Jesus introduces Himself to the church's leadership (the angel/messenger) in a most spectacular way.

First as *holy*. Peter recognized Christ as such, 'We believe and know that you are the Holy One of God' (John 6:69, NIV). Even the demons believed: 'I know who you are—the Holy One of God' (Mark 1:24). Christ's holiness points directly to his deity (cf. Isaiah 6:3 with John 12:41), as well as to His desired character for the church (Ephesians 5:26-27). The Head exemplifies the purity demanded of the body.

Next, Jesus pictures Himself as *true*. In Revelation 6:10 the martyrs under the altar cry out, 'How long Sovereign Lord, holy and true, until you judge the inhabitants of the earth and avenge our blood?' (NIV). Jesus characterized Himself as truth (John 14:6). Elsewhere John wrote: '... and we are in Him who is true, in his Son Jesus Christ. This is the true God and eternal life' (1 John 5:20). The Lord of the church is no counterfeit or bogus fanatic, but rather the real one, as well as being the holy one. Because Christ is true, He has the right to demand that the church be true also.

Third, Christ *holds the key of David*. Isaiah 22:15-23 provides the background for this imagery: 'Then I will set the key of the house of David on his shoulder, when he opens no one will shut, when he shuts no one will open' (verse 22). Eliakim was about to inherit the authority of Sheba which was symbolized by 'the key of the house of David'. The key pointed to authority, with the unique ability to open and shut doors.

Christ reminds the leaders that He has Messianic authority, undergirded by the Davidic promise as given by His heavenly Father: 'All authority has been given to Me in heaven and on earth ' (Matthew 28:18; see 2 Samuel 7:14-15). Christ's keys open doors that no one can close and shut doors that no one can open. No-one else has these keys. Christ alone possesses sovereign authority to advance His kingdom and build His church. He calls the shots and orchestrates its timing.

The Lord of the church has just pictured Himself as:

- pure in holy character
- perfect in unblemished truth
- powerful in sovereign authority

In light of Christ's following commendation for Philadelphia, it is clear He sensed pleasure over the church and felt comfortable in the midst of this model flock. They surely were holy and true; they submitted to His authority.

Commendation (3:8-10)

Affirmation (3:8)

Philadelphia wasn't threatened when Christ wrote, 'I know your deeds.' He focused on three noticeable qualities in the church.

First, they had not denied Christ's name. They, like the Christians at Antioch (Acts 11:26), were eager to be openly known as Christians. They were not secret Christians. They did not fear possible consequences for their faith, so they were not afraid to acknowledge the One in whom they believed.

Secondly, they kept Christ's Word. They took His Great Commission seriously: '... teaching them to observe all that I commanded you' (Matthew 28:20). They desired God's blessing which He promised for obedience (Revelation 1:3). Like obedient children do to their parents, the Philadelphia church brought great joy to their heavenly Father.

Finally, they had a little power. They were not the 'heavyweight' or 'super' church. In the strength category they were not significantly impressive. Why then did Christ choose to make a positive note about something that is average at best? Paul suggests the answer in 1 Corinthians 1:26-29 (NIV):

Brothers, think of what you were when you were called. Not many of you were wise by human standards; not many were influential; not many were of noble birth. But God chose the foolish things of the world to shame the wise; God chose the weak things of the world to shame the strong. He chose the lowly things of this world and the despised things—and the things that are not—to nullify the things that are, so that no one may boast before Him.

Later Paul notes personally, 'Therefore, I will boast all the more gladly about my weaknesses, so that Christ's power may rest on me' (2 Corinthians 12:9, NIV). Whatever God did through a church with little strength of its own would be acknowledged for God's glory, and not the church's. The church could not boast in its own accomplishments but only in the fact that God walked in their midst and accomplished powerful things through them. Philadelphia experienced the true life that Sardis claimed but lacked.

Why did Christ bless Philadelphia with uncloseable open doors and unopenable closed doors? Because the believers proclaimed His Name, obeyed His word and were strong enough to do a little which became much when the sovereign hand of Christ touched their work in power. In them, God received great honour.

Philadelphia also stands in contrast to the church at Smyrna. While they shared the distinction of being the only two churches who exclusively received commendation, they differed at some points. At Smyrna the door was closed, not open (2:9-10). Christ performed a sovereign act of power on behalf of the Philadelphia church, but not for Smyrna.

What is this 'door'? In Acts 14:27 Paul reported to the church at Antioch how God had opened the door of faith to the Gentiles. Paul later writes that a great door of effective work opened to him at Ephesus (1 Corinthians 16:9). He asked the Colossians to pray that God would open a door for the gospel message (Colossians 4:3). The 'door' seems best understood as a door of effective gospel ministry.

Philadelphia and Smyrna did have two things in common.

Not only were they both commended without rebuke, but their cities each housed a synagogue of Satan (2:9, 3:9). However, these similarities aside, their experience differed greatly. Those in Smyrna knew tribulation, poverty and blasphemy; they suffered, were incarcerated and faced death. Philadelphia experienced few, if any, of these traumas. On the other hand, Philadelphia had an open door. Even the enemy would bow in defeat (3:9) and the church would be kept from an hour of great testing (3:10).

Same kind of churches, same general geographical location, same time in history, but they were totally different in their experiences. Can you imagine the leadership of both churches comparing notes? They surely would have asked, 'Why?' Then they would remember that the Chief Shepherd held the keys of David. Christ controlled the door of opportunity. The timing and substance of service is controlled by Christ, the sovereign Lord of His churches. He, not the churches, writes the script. The leaders could find tremendous solace in this truth, and take great comfort while doing the bidding of their Master.

Vindication (3:9)

What are these synagogues of Satan? They were those who gathered in the name of God as Jews but were not true Jews, and thus were categorized by God as liars. They claimed to be the true assembly, but in fact were counterfeit. Paul says a true Jew is not one who is Jewish outwardly but rather inwardly (Romans 2:28-29). It is a matter of the heart not the flesh. Like the Jews of John 8:31-37 who claimed they were descendants of Abraham, the unredeemed Jews of Philadelphia were actually of their father the devil (8:44).

When Jews met they called themselves 'the assembly of

the LORD' (Numbers 16:3; 20:4; 31:16). Because they resisted and rejected the truth of Jesus as Messiah, they served Satan rather than God. Not only were there synagogues of Satan in Philadelphia and Smyrna, they were also in Jerusalem, Pisidian Antioch, Lystra, Iconium and Thessalonica (Acts 4-7; 13; 14; 17), just to mention a few. Today, churches which claim to be Christian but reject God's Word, refuse Christ's Lordship and otherwise deny Christ are modern day 'synagogues of Satan'.

While the opposition is formidable, it is not to be feared. At first glance, Philadelphia appears to be an over-achiever and Smyrna an under-achiever; but in the end God provides them both with victory (2:10; 3:9).

It is paradoxical that a Jew would bow down to a predominantly Gentile church. In the Old Testament it was just the opposite. However, here the false bow down to the true for God's glory. While this might be uncomfortable from an ethnic perspective, it is a vindication of God's power in redemption (Romans 11:11-32).

Is this bowing down future or present? Seemingly, it is both. The fact that there was an open door presently in Philadelphia would point to the present. Perhaps in Philadelphia many Jews would come to know Christ personally through seeing God's love manifest in the lives of Philadelphian believers.

Yet, elsewhere Paul writes that in the future there will be another time of submission, to Christ directly.

Therefore God exalted him to the highest place and gave him the name that is above every name, that at the name of Jesus every knee should bow, in heaven and on earth and under the earth, and every tongue confess that Jesus Christ is Lord, to the glory of God the Father (Philippians 2:9-11).

Protection (3:10)

Not only will the Philadelphia church be affirmed and vindicated, but they will also be protected. Why? Because they kept Christ's command to endure patiently. They followed Christ's example when he resisted Satan's temptation (Matthew 4:1-11). Jesus also endured the trauma of Gethsemane (Matthew 26:34-46) and for the joy set before Him, He endured the cross (Hebrews 12:2). Because of their perseverance, the Philadelphians received a fantastic promise: 'I will also keep you from the hour of testing, that hour which is about to come upon the whole world to test those who dwell upon the earth' (3:10).

When will this hour be? I believe it to be a prophetic announcement, for two reasons. First the testing is worldwide, not local. A time such as Revelation 6:10-17 describes has not yet been experienced in the world. Most importantly, the phrase 'the whole world' is used prominently in Revelation to refer to the earth's entire population during the seven year Tribulation period (6:10; 8:13; 11:10; 13:8; 13:12;13:14; 14:6; 17:2; 17:8).

Does God's promise 'to keep' mean *protection during* that hour or *prevention from entering* that hour? I would suggest that the verb/preposition combination 'keep out' grammatically and logically demands to be understood as a promise that the Philadelphians will not enter this hour of testing. One writer has said, 'The most natural way to understand "to be kept" from something which is worldwide is not to be preserved through but to be kept from being present when it happens'.

What will the hour test? A person's spiritual allegiance, whether it be to God or to Satan, not unlike Smyrna's testing (2:10). During this time there will be diabolical deceit and divine delusion like never before (2 Thessalonians 2:9-12). Satan's goal will be to deceive the world (Revelation 20:8) and to gain for himself their worship (Revelation 13:1-18).

Revelation 3:10 becomes a key biblical verse to help understand the time of the rapture. If Philadelphia, representative of all churches, is promised that they will not enter Daniel's seventieth week period, then how will God fulfill this? The most satisfactory answer is by a pretribulation rapture (cf. John 14:1-3; 1 Thessalonians 4:13-18; 1 Corinthians 15:50-57). Believers will be removed from the earth by God prior to that time of trouble.[1]

Challenge (3:11-13)

Christ reminds the believers in Philadelphia that sooner or later (His emphasis is on sooner) things will change—He will intervene (3:11). In light of coming reinforcements, Christ, the church's commander-in-chief, orders 'Do not retreat! Hold on firmly to what you have!' He gave this same advice to the saints at Thyatira (2:25).

Why? So that their crown would not be removed. Back in Revelation 2:10 I identified the crown of life, promised to Smyrna, as symbolizing the reality of salvation. Since true salvation is eternal and cannot be lost, what then does Jesus mean here? I believe he speaks not of the reality of salvation, but rather the reward of salvation. Similarly, John elsewhere warns, 'Watch out that you do not lose what you have worked for, but that you may be rewarded fully' (2 John 8, NIV).

The list of God's promises offered to the overcomer grows with the addition of four more rewards (3:12).

First, there is a focus on God's *workmanship* in salvation. The overcomer will be a pillar in God's temple, which speaks of permanence and its corollary—importance. It results in a personal emphasis whereby the overcomer will forever be in the presence of God because 'he will not go out from it any more.'

Ownership is addressed next. The name of God will be written on the overcomer. He will be branded with God's mark for eternity. Just as the followers of Satan were marked with 666 (Revelation 13:16-18), so God's people will be identified by God's name.

Third, *citizenship* appears in the use of the name of God's city—the new Jerusalem. John later takes two entire chapters (21-22) to elaborate on the holy city of God in which true believers will reside for eternity.

Finally, Christ promises an *enduring relationship*. Christ's new name will also be written on the overcomer, because Christ bought us with a price—His precious blood (1 Corinthians 6:19-20; 1 Peter 1:18-19). I believe the name here is also mentioned as 'the name no one knows except Himself' in Revelation 19:12. Most likely this is the name that embodies the hundreds of different individual names given to Christ in Scripture. This one name would express every aspect of His infinite character.

With such promises, who would not want to listen carefully to this grand letter? In case someone misses the importance of the message, Christ sends a reminder, 'He who has an ear, let him hear what the Spirit says to the churches' (3:13).

Summing Up

Philadelphia proves to be a noteworthy church. Though its appearance was not spectacular, Philadelphia's faithfulness shows us the power of a congregation that pleases Christ. The following features make it a church well worth our careful observation and emulation.

1. Commitment to holy living (3:7)
2. Commitment to truth (3:7)
3. Commitment to Christ's sovereignty (3:7-8)
4. Commitment to obedience (3:8)
5. Commitment to proclamation (3:8)
6. Commitment to maximum effort (3:8-9)
7. Commitment to finishing what they started (3:10)

Every committed church of Jesus Christ should pray regularly, 'Lord, build Your church, not on the strength of our flesh, but through the door which Christ opens and the power which Your Spirit provides. Amen.'

8

LAODICEA
THE USELESS CHURCH

And to the angel of the church in Laodicea write:

The Amen, the faithful and true Witness, the Beginning of the creation of God, says this: 'I know your deeds, that you are neither cold nor hot; I would that you were cold or hot. So because you are lukewarm, and neither hot nor cold, I will spit you out of My mouth. Because you say, "I am rich, and have become wealthy, and have need of nothing," and you do not know that you are wretched and miserable and poor and blind and naked, I advise you to buy from Me gold refined by fire, that you may become rich, and white garments, that you may clothe yourself, and that the shame of your nakedness may not be revealed; and eye salve to anoint your eyes, that you may see.

'Those whom I love, I reprove and discipline; be zealous therefore, and repent. Behold, I stand at the door and knock; if anyone hears My voice and opens the door, I will come in to him, and will dine with him, and he with Me.

'He who overcomes, I will grant to him to sit down with Me on My throne, as I also overcame and sat down with My Father on His throne. He who has an ear, let him hear what the Spirit says to the churches (Revelation 3:14-22).

Christ's seventh letter to the churches of Asia turns out to be the epitome of heavenly nastygrams. It unsparingly condemns the church at Laodicea.

Only forty miles separated Philadelphia and Laodicea physically, but spiritually the distance was great, such were the opposing qualities of their churches. Philadelphia, the 'obedient' church, is grimly distinguished from the church at Laodicea which is about to be abandoned by God because of its sickening taste.

Laodicea holds the distinction of being the only church of the seven about which Christ has absolutely nothing good to say. Even Sardis, the 'dying' church, had a few people whose white garments had not been soiled. The church could be described as sentimental, skin deep, flabby, anaemic, proud, humanly respectable, secular and self-sufficient, which Christ finds nauseating. Humanly speaking, we cringe at the Lord's severity in condemning the Laodicean church, but his comments only emphasize the inviolable nature of His Word and will for His church.

Laodicea was located in close proximity to two other cities mentioned in the New Testament—Colosse and Hierapolis (Colossians 4:13). Several decades earlier Laodicea had received a letter from Paul which is not included in the New Testament (some believe it to be Philemon, cf. Colossians 4:16). That letter was also to be sent to Colossae just as the Colossian letter was sent to Laodicea.

Wealth characterized Laodicea's economy. For example, when it suffered severe earthquake damage in AD 60, the city rebuilt from its own financial resources without asking Rome for help. The church had become a reflection of the city, thinking they were able to operate independently of God.

Commission (3:14)

Christ comes to the leadership of the church as an Accuser, not their Advocate. Before he reads the indictment, Christ apparently anticipates a possible arrogant response such as, 'Who do you think you are?' The Chief Shepherd's credentials unimpeachably earn Him the right to throw the book at this sad excuse for a church. Jesus focuses on three of His characteristics which establish Him as truth incarnate.

First, He is *the Amen*. 'Amen' is a term used to affirm truth (1 Chronicles 16:36; Nehemiah 5:13; 8:6). Isaiah refers to the Lord as 'the God of truth' (65:16); so Paul could write that because of Christ there is an Amen to the promises of God (2 Corinthians 1:20). Christ as the Amen becomes the verification and ultimate authentication of truth. Jesus is the last word on truth because He is the truth (John 14:6).

Next, He is *the faithful and true witness*. These words also describe Christ elsewhere in Revelation (1:5; 3:7; 19:11). He is true in that His witness is inerrant, and He is faithful because His words are infallibly trustworthy. As Head of the church who walks in the midst of the lampstands (1:13), Christ is the perfect eyewitness and thus the repository of truth.

Third, Jesus describes Himself as *the ruler (arche) of God's creation*. Elsewhere He is described as 'the Alpha and the Omega, the First and the Last, the Beginning and the End' (Revelation 22:13). All things came into being through Him and without Him nothing has come into being that now exists (John 1:3). So Christ is the source of truth by virtue of being the Creator.

As the last word on truth, the repository of truth and the source of truth, Jesus Christ qualifies as the most reliable commentator on the state of affairs within the Laodicean church. His testimony need not be cross-examined or challenged. Since the Laodicean church had nothing to be commended, Christ starts out with His indictment.

Condemnation (3:15-17)
Christ uses two elements of local life to illustrate his distaste for the church. The first is taken from their natural resources and the second is in relationship to the local economy.

Known by Jesus, their deeds marked them out as neither cold (literally 'icy cold') nor hot (literally 'boiling'), but rather lukewarm or tepid. Thus, Christ threatens to spit them out of His mouth (3:15-16). By this act He will remove Himself and His spiritual blessing from the church. Thus, in one generation, it could be spiritually dead.

The images used here would have been vividly clear to the Laodiceans who lived nearby two special sources of water. Hierapolis had pools of hot medicinal springs and Colossae contributed pure, cold waters.

Lukewarm water had little, if any, value. So Laodicea was neither hot in the sense of being therapeutically healing for the spiritually sick nor cool and refreshing for the spiritually weary. The church proved to be tepidly ineffective and therefore distasteful to their Lord. They were taken to task for their barrenness of deeds which neither restored nor refreshed in a spiritual sense. The church literally made Jesus want to vomit.

Then Jesus turns to the local economy to make a point. Someone in Laodicea might resort to elaborating on the church's wealth and self-sufficiency to counter the lukewarm charge. But it is unimportant what the community says of a church (like in Sardis, cf. 3:1) or what a church says about itself, as is the case here. Jesus will give them the truth, the whole truth and nothing but the truth.

Generally speaking, the Laodicean church proved to be wretched and pitiful by God's standard. More specifically, the church could be characterized as poor, blind and naked. Materialism had so undermined them spiritually that they were about to cave in under the weight of their self-indulgence.

Economically, Laodicea was a notable banking centre. It did not even need the help of Rome in a crisis. But because the church believed they did not need God, Jesus declares them to be in a state of spiritual poverty.

Medically, this city had a great reputation. It housed a famous medical school where doctors were so well known that some of their names (Zeuxis and Alexander Philalethes) appeared on local coins. 'Phrygia powder' was exported worldwide from Laodicea as a salve for eyes and ears. Laodicea was busy making a reputation for restoring physical sight to the blind, but the church there didn't even realize they had become spiritually blind.

This city also excelled in the manufacturing of clothes. It was especially famous for its soft, violet-black, glossy wool. So proud were these church members of how they dressed others, it did not dawn on them that they were spiritually naked. They remind us of the well-known tale by Hans Christian Anderson, 'The Emperor's New Clothes'.

The church lacked spiritual discernment, being similar in this respect to the church in Corinth (1 Corinthians 2:12-3:3), and parallelled the spiritually immoral church to which James wrote: 'You adulterous people, don't you know that friendship with the world is hatred towards God? Anyone who chooses to be a friend of the world becomes an enemy of God' (James 4:4, NIV).

This raises a very important question. Is this a non-church

filled with unbelievers or a genuine church comprised primarily of immature, fleshly Christians? Several hints in the text suggest that, regardless of the repugnant nature of the church, it was an authentic church. These include the following facts:

1. Christ stands in their midst (1:13).
2. Both the obedient and disobedient assemblies are called churches (cf. 1:4, 11 and 3:7 with 3:14).
3. The term 'wretched' (3:17) is used by Paul of himself (Romans 7:24).
4. 'Blind' is used of believers (2 Peter 1:9).

There are times when believers can appear to be like unbelievers (1 Corinthians 3:3). That is why Paul later tells the Corinthians: 'Examine yourselves to see whether you are in the faith; test yourselves. Do you not realize that Christ Jesus is in you—unless, of course, you fail the test?' (2 Corinthians 13:5). There is no doubt that some of the Laodiceans did fail the test, but not all of them. Here, Laodicea represents a church which has deteriorated greatly from its once pure state and thus brought the greatest measure of displeasure to its Founder.

Most interestingly, Satan is alluded to or mentioned directly in five of the seven letters (2: 2, 9, 13, 24; 3:9). But in both letters to churches worthy of condemnation—only Sardis and Laodicea—the full weight of responsibility for sin rests entirely on the shoulders of the churches. Satan is not mentioned in either letter. They have no-one to blame but themselves and are therefore justly held accountable by Christ.

Confrontation (3:18-20)

Can a church which has lost its usefulness to Christ ever regain it? Here the church's Head masterfully expresses the fulness of His mercy and grace to a church which by human standards is beyond forgiveness. Restoration is possible—if the leaders will submit to God's direction. 'I counsel you' translates best to 'Do it my way or else!' Christ's plan involved the Laodiceans obtaining from Him what they actually lacked spiritually but thought they already had.

How were they 'to buy' their things? On the physical side they had bought till they needed no more. However, due to spiritual bankruptcy they had nothing with which to bargain. That's where God's grace takes over. Their poverty would force them to come to God on His terms for they had nothing to offer in themselves. Future spiritual blessing will only be obtained by the price of repentance, like the tax-collector who cried out, 'God, be merciful to me, the sinner' (Luke 18:13).

The ultimate riches of God are found only in the fullness of spiritual maturity and in the entirety of God's Word. The Laodiceans had failed to value these in God's economy.

> Therefore, my brothers, be all the more eager to make your calling and election sure. For if you do these things, you will never fall, and you will receive a rich welcome into the eternal kingdom of our Lord and Saviour Jesus Christ (2 Peter 1:10-11, NIV).

> Because I love your commands more than gold, more than pure gold ... (Psalm 119:127, NIV).

White garments are the robes of righteousness (Revelation 7:13-14). These can be in a Christian's possession, but he does not necessarily always wear them. That is why Paul tells the

Ephesians to put on the breastplate of righteousness (Ephesians 6:14). This same kind of injunction is given to believers by using the clothing illustration to picture their new self: 'put on the new self, created to be like God in true righteousness and holiness' (Ephesians 4:24, NIV).

Eye salve is needed for spiritual discernment. The Laodiceans were like those to whom Peter wrote, 'But if anyone does not have them, he is nearsighted and blind, and has forgotten that he has been cleansed from his past sins' (2 Peter 1:9, NIV). Paul uses this same picture when dealing with the Galatians, 'You foolish Galatians, who has bewitched you, before whose eyes Jesus Christ was publicly portrayed as crucified' (Galatians 3:1).

Now here is the only positive element in the whole letter. There could be only one thing worse for the Laodiceans than the stinging rebuke of this letter. That would be to have no letter at all. This letter is evidence of Christ's love for the church and His desire for it to be restored. To reprove and discipline is to love. To ignore is to hate (cf. Proverbs 13:24), '... because the Lord disciplines those he loves, and he punishes everyone he accepts as a son. Endure hardship as discipline; God is treating you as sons. For what son is not disciplined by his father?' (Hebrews 12:6-7, NIV). Christ invites the Laodiceans to turn energetically from their own ways to the ways of God—or in other words, 'to repent!'

This same concept is now presented in a different way. Revelation 3:20 brings to mind Holman Hunt's painting 'The Light of the World'. This portrait has often been thought to picture salvation. While it could be appropriate, the context suggests that it pictures Christ standing at the door of his church seeking to come back in.

It would be like a rich man inviting a beggar to come and

live in his house and share his riches. With the passing of time, the beggar rudely evicts the rich man from his own home. So the rich man then tries to regain entrance into his own home. This is the picture of Christ graciously seeking to regain His presence and prominence in the Laodicean church.

There is another feature of the text that reinforces this idea. Greeks normally ate three meals. Breakfast was called *akratisma* and consisted of dried bread dipped in wine. The noon meal, or *aristion*, involved a picnic snack eaten along the way. The evening meal, or *deipnon,* served as the main meal. Christ promised the *deipnon* to the Laodiceans. Christ offers this full meal, and the fellowship experience that went with it, to the beggarly Laodiceans who were suffering from spiritual malnutrition. Christ, far more than did the Laodiceans, desires for Himself and for them the fulness of spiritual intimacy in the church.

Challenge (3:21-22)

As always, Christ's letter ends on a note of hope. What is presently Christ's heavenly experience will be given to the overcomers in the future. He now sits at the right hand of the Father.

'I will grant to him to sit down with Me on My throne.' This broad statement summarizes all of the particular over- comer promises in the previous six letters. We will participate in the Father and Son experience of ruling from heaven's throne (cf. Revelation 20:6).

Here is a summary of the specific overcomer promises from the seven letters.

1. Eating from the tree of life (2:7).
2. The crown of life (2:10).
3. Protection from the second death (2:11).

4.   Hidden manna (2:17).
5.   A white stone with a new name (2:17).
6.   To rule over the nations (2:26-27).
7.   The morning star (2:28).
8.   Clothed in white garments (3:5).
9.   A place in the book of life (3:5).
10. Christ's confession in heaven (3:5).
11. To become a pillar in God's temple (3:12).
12. To become identified with God's name (3:12)
13. To become identified with the New Jerusalem (3:12)
14. To become identified with Christ's new name (3:12).
15. The right to sit with Christ on his heavenly throne (3:21).

These promises are so wonderful that Christ ends, as He does each of the seven letters, with an appeal for the churches to hear with a listening ear. 'He who has an ear, let him hear what the Spirit says to the churches' (3:22). Twentieth century churches need to hear, listen, and obey.

The Laodicean profile
How will we recognize a Laodicean type church? What characterizes a church which deserves such drastic words? Could you possibly be in this kind of church?

Eight sharply defined qualities are evidence of this kind of notorious church. Just the opposite marks out Christ's kind of church.

1. Focusing more on religious trends and theories than on the Truth (3:14).

2. Focusing more on being religiously neutral and accom-

modating than on being committed to the fundamentals of the faith (3:15-16).

3. Focusing more on self-sufficiency than on God-dependency (3:17).

4. Focusing more on money than on Scripture (3:17-18).

5. Focusing more on fashions than on holy living (3:17-18).

6. Focusing more on understanding the world than on understanding God (3:17-18).

7. Focusing more on contemporary relevance than on spiritual repentance (3:19).

8. Focusing more on the presence of civic and religious dignitaries than on the presence of the Lord Jesus Christ (3:20).

A final note

Christ wrote seven letters to the seven churches. While they were all different, Christ loved each one enough to write and tell them what He thought. Since Christ's wisdom for the church is timeless in nature, these epistles become the basis for twentieth century churches to evaluate themselves and make changes where Christ calls for them. To do less is to reject Christ's authority over the church and ignore His promise of blessing for obedience (1:3).

As a reminder, here is how the Chief Shepherd viewed the churches of Asia Minor. He looks at the twentieth century church through the same eyes and with an identical mind.

Ephesus	The Lost-love Church
Smyrna	The Suffering Church
Pergamum	The Compromising Church
Thyatira	The Tolerating Church
Sardis	The Dying Church
Philadelphia	The Obedient Church
Laodicea	The Useless Church

PART TWO

THE CHURCHES OF GREECE

Similar to Christ's seven letters to seven churches, Paul wrote to churches in seven distinct regions or cities (Colossae, Corinth, Ephesus, Galatia, Philippi, Rome, Thessalonica). Three of these churches have been selected for our study because their letters include more details than do the others. We begin with Paul's two letters to the church at Thessalonica.

9

**THESSALONICA
THE REPRODUCING CHURCH**

You also became imitators of us and of the Lord, having received the word in much tribulation with the joy of the Holy Spirit, so that you became an example to all the believers in Macedonia and Achaia. For the word of the Lord has sounded forth from you, not only in Macedonia and Achaia, but also in every place your faith toward God has gone forth, so that we have no need to say anything (1 Thessalonians 1:6-8).

Thessalonica lies near the ancient site of Therma on the Thermaic Gulf at the northern reaches of the Aegean Sea. This city became the principle capital of Macedonia around 168 BC and enjoyed the status of a *free city* which was ruled by its own citizenry (Acts 17:6) as a part of the Roman Empire.

Thessalonica served as the centre of political and commercial activity in Macedonia, being ideally located along the east-west highway called 'Via Egnatia'. The city was known as 'the mother of all Macedonia'. The population in Paul's day numbered about 200,000 people.

Paul and his co-workers had originally travelled a hundred miles from Philippi, by way of Amphipolis and Apollonia, to Thessalonica during Paul's second missionary journey (ca. AD 50, Acts 16:1-18:21). Upon his arrival he sought out a synagogue in which to teach, as was his custom. Here he dialogued with the Jews using Old Testament Scriptures which pointed to Christ's death and resurrection, in order to prove that Jesus of Nazareth was truly the Jewish Messiah. His converts came from among the Jews, Hellenistic proselytes and some wealthy women of the community (Acts 17:1-4). Numbered among the converts were Jason (Acts 17:5), Gaius (Acts 19:28), Aristarchus and Secundus (Acts 20:4).

Because of their effective ministry, the Jews evicted Paul's team from the city and they went south to Berea (Acts 17:5-10). There Paul had a similar experience of opposition, and thus left for Athens while Silvanus (Silas) and Timothy stayed behind (Acts 17:11-14). They rejoined Paul in Athens (Acts 17:15-16; cf. 1 Thessalonians 3:1), from where Timothy was later dispatched back to Thessalonica (1 Thessalonians 3:2). Afterwards, Silvanus apparently travelled from Athens to Philippi, while Paul journeyed on alone to Corinth (Acts

18:1). After Timothy and Silvanus rejoined Paul in Corinth (Acts 18:5), Paul wrote his first epistle to the Thessalonians.

This is the first of Paul's two known letters to the church at Thessalonica. It is dated ca. AD 51. This date is archaeologically verified by an inscription in the temple of Apollos at Delphi, near Corinth, that dates Gallio's service as proconsul in Achaia to ca. AD 51-52 (see Acts 18:12-17). If Paul's letter to the churches of Galatia was his first, then this is his second canonical epistle.

Paul's reasons for writing flowed from his shepherd's heart which was concerned about the flock from which he had been separated. Some of Paul's purposes clearly include:

encouraging the church (1:2-10)
answering false allegations (2:1-12)
comforting the persecuted church (2:13-16)
expressing his joy in their faith (2:17-3:13)
reminding them of the importance of moral purity (4:1-8)
condemning the sluggard's lifestyle (4:9-12)
correcting a misunderstanding of future events (4:13-5:11)
defusing tensions within the flock (5:12-15)
exhorting them in the basics of Christian living (5:16-22)

In summary, Paul writes to these believers to strengthen their early steps in the Christian life, so that he could complete what was lacking in their faith (3:10). 1 Thessalonians is a compassionate letter written to a consecrated church.

Most likely Paul was still in Corinth when he wrote his second epistle. Some have suggested that Paul penned it from Ephesus (Acts 18:18-21), but his eighteen-month stay in Corinth provided ample time for a follow-up letter to be authored. Paul apparently was aware of the happenings in

Thessalonica through correspondence or couriers. The church had become more effective (1:3), but the pressure and persecution had enlarged as well. So Paul wrote to his beloved flock which had been discouraged by persecution (chapter 1), deceived by false teachers (chapter 2) and disobedient to Paul's commands (chapter 3). In all likelihood, this letter followed in late AD 51 or early 52, three to six months after the first letter to Thessalonians.

Paul writes a concerned letter to bolster a church which is growing in the midst of painful trials. The purposes of this second epistle are to comfort a persecuted church (1:3-12), to correct a frightened and falsely taught church about the future (2:1-15) and to confront a disobedient and undisciplined church (3:6-15).

The Model Shepherd

Few would disagree that, humanly speaking, Paul served as a shepherd extraordinaire to many congregations, including Thessalonica, Philippi, and Corinth. The Pauline epistles, along with Acts 13-28, biographically describe the pastoral priorities established by Paul as he laboured to extend the church from Jerusalem to Rome.

In Revelation 1:12-20 we discovered the unique features that Christ brought to the church as her Chief Shepherd. Undershepherds would do well to emulate the example of Paul. Just as each of the seven churches of Asia had a messenger or 'leader of leaders', so every church requires good pastoral leadership which will pattern its human efforts after Paul's example.

We must recognize the direct relationship between the quality of leadership in the church and the quality of ministry in the church. The writer of Hebrews put it best:

Remember those who led you, who spoke the word of God to you; and considering the result of their conduct, imitate their faith (Hebrews 13:7).

Obey your leaders, and submit to them; for they keep watch over your souls, as those who will give an account. Let them do this with joy and not with grief, for this would be unprofitable for you (Hebrews 13:17).

Paul's ministry profile in 1 and 2 Thessalonians outlines the essential elements of effective pastoral ministry. His life among the church illustrates what a shepherd is to be and to do according to God's will. The following summary of responsibilities describes Paul's ministry among the Thessalonians.

1.	Praying	1 Thessalonians 1:2-3; 3:9-13; 2 Thessalonians 2:16-17
2.	Evangelizing	1 Thessalonians 1:4-5, 9-10
3.	Equipping	1 Thessalonians 1:6-8
4.	Defending	1 Thessalonians 2:1-6
5.	Loving	1 Thessalonians 2:7-8
6.	Labouring	1 Thessalonians 2:9
7.	Modelling	1 Thessalonians 2:10
8.	Leading	1 Thessalonians 2:11-12
9.	Feeding	1 Thessalonians 2:13
10.	Suffering	1 Thessalonians 2:14-20
11.	Watching	1 Thessalonians 3:1-8
12.	Warning	1 Thessalonians 4:1-8
13.	Teaching	1 Thessalonians 4:9-5:11
14.	Exhorting	1 Thessalonians 5:12-24
15.	Encouraging	2 Thessalonians 1:3-12
16.	Correcting	2 Thessalonians 2:1-12
17.	Rebuking	2 Thessalonians 3:6, 14
18.	Rescuing	2 Thessalonians 3:15

It would be difficult to imagine that a pastor could do any less than this and still be effective. Conversely, if a pastor took these responsibilities seriously, one cannot imagine the pastor having time to do much more. These various aspects of Paul's pastoral ministry exemplify the top priorities for each succeeding generation.

Because of Paul's strong sense of pastoral responsibility to God for the church and because of his deep love for the flock, he wrote these two letters as an extension of his ministry to them. Although he could not be with them, he nevertheless consistently thought of the church and desired that they excel. In these letters we discover what the Apostle, by God's direction, commends and condemns at Thessalonica.

Paul's Commendations

The apostle's intimate correspondence to the church, which he dearly loves, exposes us to the basic fibre of the Thessalonian church. These letters let us look below the surface and probe the very heart of the church.

For the most part, these two letters taken together sound much like Christ's letters to Smyrna and Philadelphia. However, there are hints that the Thessalonian church had several emerging problems that needed to be corrected quickly. So let's look first at those features for which the Apostle Paul had nothing but praise, and then his concerns.

Committed Church

To each of the seven churches of Asia, Christ remarked, 'I know your works'. Just as He commended the church at Ephesus for her 'deeds', 'toil' and 'perseverance', Paul commends the Thessalonians for their work, labour and steadfastness (1 Thessalonians 1:2-3). The same three Greek words are used in both instances to describe these two churches.

'Faith' in Christ had produced works, just as God had designed the outcome of salvation: 'For we are His workmanship, created in Christ Jesus for good works, which God prepared beforehand, that we should walk in them' (Ephesians 2:10). As newly redeemed bondservants, they gladly worked on behalf of their Lord Jesus.

'Love' for Christ took their works to a deeper level called labour or toil. Because of Christ's sacrifice on their behalf, they now sacrificed on His behalf. They spared nothing in their spiritual service, always working to the point of exhaustion.

'Hope' toward Christ's return produced the ultimate level of commitment: steadfastness or perseverance. They would stay with their kingdom labour on earth until their Lord and Master called them away to be with Him in heaven. They would be found at their Christ-appointed labour until the end.

The Thessalonians committed themselves to gospel service. Not satisfied with ordinary or average work, they laboured long and hard on Christ's behalf. They intended to do this as long as it pleased Christ.

Their commitment proved genuine. After Paul sent Timothy to strengthen them, he returned with a wonderful report of their 'faith and love' (1 Thessalonians 3:6). Even more telling, Paul commends the Thessalonians in his second letter because their faith was greatly enlarged and their love for one another had grown greater (1:3).

Submitted Church
'You also became imitators of us and of the Lord' (1 Thessalonians 1:6). As Hebrews 13:7 exhorts, the Thessalonians imitated the faith of their spiritual father and his associates.

They lived out Paul's admonition to the Corinthian church: 'Be imitators of me, just as I also am of Christ' (1 Corinthians 11:1).

As children submit to and obey their father and mother, so did the Thessalonians to their spiritual parents. But the Thessalonians' submission went a step further. They would have found it easy to submit in good times, however, their submission also came in a time of persecution and hardship.

Paul notes that they received the Word in much tribulation (1 Thessalonians 1:6). The church began with instant spiritual conflict (Acts 17:1-9) and seemingly never knew a moment of peace, but continued in persecution. In spite of these obstacles and distractions, the church suffered the same way as did the churches of Judea earlier (1 Thessalonians 2:14). They were submissive at the highest level.

Reproducing Church

The Thessalonians took Christ's Great Commission seriously (Matthew 28:18-20). Having first been an example to other believers, they then spread the gospel wherever they went (1 Thessalonians 1:7-8). The gospel spread in the city of Thessalonica, the region of Macedonia and beyond to Achaia, and wherever else the Thessalonians travelled beyond their own natural boundaries.

Although the text does not explicitly say so, a little sanctified imagination can picture the Thessalonians discipling other believers and evangelizing unbelievers. Undoubtedly other churches came into being because of their spreading the gospel.

Repentant Church

The Thessalonians had turned from the false to the true God in their salvation (1 Thessalonians 1:9). Their 180 degree turn, spiritually speaking, involved completely turning away from idols and completely turning toward God (Acts 11:18; 2 Corinthians 7:10).

Unlike the church at Sardis, which claimed to be alive although Jesus declared her to be dead, the Thessalonian church had actually been dead but was now alive. They had been converted by gospel preaching (1 Thessalonians 1:5), then opposed false religion rather than participated in it (Acts 17:5-9) and openly declared their allegiance to the Lord Jesus Christ (1 Thessalonians 1:8).

Serving Church

The Thessalonians understood that service to God fitted their new status of being Christians (1 Thessalonians 1:9). Christ is Lord and they were his servants. While they remained on earth, they were not to attempt to make God their servant or indulge themselves in the wealth of the world. Rather, they now would serve God rather than mammon (Matthew 6:24).

Paul's example had been to serve the Lord (Acts 20:19). He instructed the Colossian church, 'It is the Lord Christ whom you serve' (Colossians 3:24). When one had a perfect Master, the only reasonable and spiritual response was to serve Him.

Patient Church

With confident expectancy, the Thessalonians awaited Jesus' return (1 Thessalonians 1:10). He promised, 'I will come again' (John 14:3). The angels proclaimed, 'This Jesus, who has been taken up from you into heaven, will come in just the same way as you have watched Him go into heaven' (Acts 1:11).

The Thessalonian church was a 'second coming' church. Their hope rested in the glorious thought that one day Christ would return and deliver them from a sin-filled world. The Thessalonian believers, like the believers on Crete, were looking for the blessed hope and the appearing of the glory of our great God and Saviour, Christ Jesus (Titus 2:13).

Accepting Church

How can we explain such radical change in people's lives as was seen in the Thessalonians? How does a church mature as fast as the Thessalonian assembly? By the power of God's Word working in them (1 Thessalonians 2:13). They began with God's Word (Acts 17:1-3) and they continued in God's Word. They didn't doubt, hesitate, accept some and reject some; rather they completely accepted Paul's message as God's message.

God's Word is the power of God to save (Romans 1:16; 1 Corinthians 1:18). God's Word is the power by which Christians grow (1 Peter 2:1-3; 2 Peter 3:18). God's Word goes forth with a promise that it will accomplish God's bidding (Isaiah 55:11). This power by which God works in us is able to do exceeding abundantly beyond all that we can ask or think (Ephesians 3:20).

What sort of work does God's Word do? Here's a sample! It

- saves (1 Peter 1:23)
- teaches (2 Timothy 3:16)
- rebukes (2 Timothy 3:16)
- corrects (2 Timothy 3:16)
- instructs (2 Timothy 3:16)
- equips (2 Timothy 3:17)

- guides (Psalm 119:105)
- counsels (Psalm 119:24)
- revives (Psalm 119:154)
- restores (Psalm 19:7)
- warns (Psalm 19:11)
- rewards (Psalm 19:11)
- nourishes (1 Peter 2:2)
- judges (Hebrews 4:12)
- sanctifies (John 17:17)
- frees (John 8:31-32)
- enriches (Colossians 3:16)
- protects (Psalm 19:11)
- strengthens (Psalm 119:28)
- makes wise (Psalm 119:97-100)
- confronts (Jeremiah 23:29)
- prospers (Psalm 1:3)

Persecuted Church

No one actively seeks out persecution. While it seemed to purify the church at Smyrna, persecution could not fully cleanse Pergamum. Suffering comes by the will of God (1 Peter 3:17; 4:19) and is not normal for all churches. But persecution quickly found the Thessalonians.

> For you, brethren, became imitators of the churches of God in Christ Jesus that are in Judea, for you also endured the same sufferings at the hands of your own countrymen, even as they did from the Jews, who both killed the Lord Jesus and the prophets, and drove us out. They are not pleasing to God, but hostile to all men, hindering us from speaking to the Gentiles, that they might be saved; with the result that they always fill up the measure of their sins. But wrath has come upon them to the utmost (1 Thessalonians 2:14-16).

Time did not diminish the pain and conflict. In his second letter Paul writes, 'therefore, we ourselves speak proudly of you among the churches of God for your perseverance and faith in the midst of all your persecutions and afflictions which you endure' (2 Thessalonians 1:4).

Suffering for righteousness' sake finds favour with God (1 Peter 2:20). Suffering as a Christian glorifies God (1 Peter 4:16); being reviled for the name of Christ brings blessing (1 Peter 4:14).

This wonderful promise awaits those who now suffer on behalf of Christ.

> And after you have suffered for a little while, the God of all grace, who called you to His eternal glory in Christ, will Himself perfect, confirm, strengthen and establish you (1 Peter 5:10).

Staunch Church

When Timothy returned to Paul, he reported that the Thessalonians were 'standing firm' (1 Thessalonians 3:8). The church had started in the midst of spiritual warfare and had grown in the same environment. They were battle hardened veterans from the beginning. Even though the church had existed for less than a year when Paul wrote, the believers exhibited maturity beyond their years.

The Thessalonians refused any spiritual retreat. They stood their ground without compromise. Because they burned their secular bridges behind them, the only way to go was forward. While the enemy would not always allow them to advance, the Thessalonians purposed not to give up the ground that had already been gained for them by Christ.

God-Pleasing Church

Obedient churches please God as did the Thessalonians (1 Thessalonians 4:1). Pleasing God is an important part of salvation's fruit.

> For it is God who is at work in you, both to will and to work for His good pleasure (Philippians 2:13).

> Now the God of peace, who brought up from the dead the great Shepherd of the sheep through the blood of the eternal covenant, even Jesus our Lord, equip you in every good thing to do His will, working in us that which is pleasing in His sight, through Jesus Christ, to whom be the glory forever and ever. Amen (Hebrews 13:20-21).

Paul's top ambition was to please the Lord (2 Corinthians 5:9). Jesus testified, 'I always do the things that are pleasing to Him' (John 8:29). The Scriptures explicitly list at least nine activities that please the Lord. Surely these would have been a consistent part of the Thessalonian church life.

1. Spiritual commitment (Romans 12:1).
2. Submission (Colossians 3:20; Titus 2:9).
3. Walking in God's will (Colossians 1:9-10).
4. Spiritual focus (1 Corinthians 7:32).
5. Purity (1 Thessalonians 4:1-3).
6. Doing good (Hebrews 13:16).
7. True worship (Psalm 69:30-31; John 4:24).
8. Living by God's Spirit (Romans 8:6).
9. Preaching the truth (1 Thessalonians 2:4).

Loving-the-brethren Church

Love is the most often mentioned 'one another' in Scripture. On at least ten other occasions the same activity is addressed

(Romans 12:10; 13:8; 1 Thessalonians 3:12; 2 Thessalonians 1:3; 1 Peter 1:22; 1 John 3:11, 23; 4:7, 11; 2 John 5).

Jesus said, 'By this all men will know that you are My disciples, if you have love for one another' (John 13:35). This contrasting truth is also taught, 'Owe nothing to anyone except to love one another; for he who loves his neighbour has fulfilled the law' (Romans 13:8).

Even as well as the Thessalonians must have been doing, Paul exhorts, 'Excel still more' (1 Thessalonians 4:10). The church needed to grow continually in love towards one another.

Praying Church

Paul had great opportunities to preach the gospel. He understood that evangelism needs to be undergirded by effective prayer. So he asked the Thessalonians to pray for his ministry that the Word of God would spread rapidly and be glorified, just as it had been in the beginning at Thessalonica (2 Thessalonians 3:1).

A more important prayer request could not have been rendered. Therefore, we can conclude that the Thessalonians had already demonstrated their faithfulness to an earnest ministry of prayer. Thus, Paul could entrust this supremely important matter to their prayer ministry.

Paul's Concerns

We don't often think of Thessalonica in the same league as Ephesus, Pergamum and Thyatira. But just as Christ both commended and condemned these three, so Paul has some words of correction for the Thessalonians.

False Teaching

They had succumbed to false teachers (2 Thessalonians 2:1-2). Apparently, some had come in the name of Paul and taught something false that the church naively believed to be true. But rather than providing comfort, it disturbed them and shook their composure.

Paul gave two rules by which to prevent this from happening again. First, remember the truth (2 Thessalonians 2:5). By comparing future teaching with already affirmed truth from the past, the true can be distinguished from the false. By setting the new alongside the true, false teaching can be exposed.

Second, be sure the message is from Scripture. Paul made a significant effort to point out the distinguishing or authenticating mark of his own handwriting (2 Thessalonians 3:17). Without this sign, no letter was to be received as a genuine apostolic letter from Paul.

Undisciplined Living

Paul had alluded to a possible problem in 1 Thessalonians 4:9-12. Apparently his instructions were ignored because later he addressed this as an escalating issue of sin in 2 Thessalonians 3:6-15.

The situation seemed to be that a group of people in the church, for unknown reasons, refused to work and take care of their own needs (2 Thessalonians 3:8, 10-12). Paul instructed the Thessalonians to deal with undisciplined idleness as sin and to initiate church discipline in order hopefully to restore these brethren to a productive life (2 Thessalonians 3:6, 14-15).

A Warning to Pastors

Even the best churches have areas of vulnerability. For Thessalonica they included (1) false teaching and (2) undisciplined living. If you were to take honest stock of your assembly, where are the weaknesses?

On the other hand, the great strengths in the church did not come without hard work and they will not last without vigilant shepherding on the part of all who are involved in leadership.

Paul's description for a healthy church reads like this:

> As apostles of Christ we could have been a burden to you, but we were gentle among you, like a mother caring for her little children. We loved you so much that we were delighted to share with you not only the gospel of God but our lives as well, because you had become so dear to us. Surely you remember, brothers, our toil and hardship; we worked night and day in order not to be a burden to anyone while we preached the gospel of God to you.
>
> You are witnesses, and so is God, of how holy, righteous and blameless we were among you who believed. For you know that we dealt with each of you as a father deals with his own children, encouraging, comforting and urging you to live lives worthy of God, who calls you into his kingdom and glory (I Thessalonians 2:6-12, NIV)

You must keep working to strengthen your strengths and shore up your weaknesses. In this, you will labour on Christ's behalf in the spirit of Paul's pastoral ministry pattern.

10

PHILIPPI
THE CARING CHURCH

If therefore there is any encouragement in Christ, if there is any consolation of love, if there is any fellowship of the Spirit, if any affection and compassion, make my joy complete by being of the same mind, maintaining the same love, united in spirit, intent on one purpose.

Do nothing from selfishness or empty conceit, but with humility of mind let each of you regard one another as more important than himself; do not merely look out for your own personal interests, but also for the interests of others (Philippians 2:1-4).

Of all the churches mentioned in our New Testament, Philippi might be the least probable, from a human perspective, to be planted, to thrive and later to receive a letter from Paul. It will quickly become apparent when reading Acts 16 that Paul did not have an intentional plan nor did he possess a step-by-step formula for planting churches. But God did; He sovereignly raised up the Philippian church according to His eternal will (Ephesians 1:4).

Knowing in advance how the Philippian church would come into being, we would probably have been inclined to rewrite the script because the story is almost too bizarre to believe. But the truth of the matter is that the church actually began as reported by Dr. Luke who was an eyewitness (note the 'we' and 'us' in Acts 16:10-17).

The city of Philippi had been founded by Philip II of Macedon, the father of Alexander the Great (ca. 350-300 BC). As reported by Luke, Philippi served as a leading city in the region, having been accorded the honour of being a Roman 'colony' (Acts 16:21).

Philippi was no mere conquered province. History had favoured her with the 'Italic right'. This exalted status made Philippi equal to any colony on Italian soil; even her residents were considered actual citizens of Rome. As such, she was exempt from the oversight of provincial governors, plus poll and property taxes. She also was strategically located on the famous 'Via Egnatia', the Roman military road that carried east-west commercial traffic from Rome to the east. Philippi enjoyed a privileged status, both politically and economically. As such, she became the important centre for a new church and the spread of the gospel into Europe.

The Beginnings

When Paul launched out on his second missionary journey (ca. AD 49-51) neither he nor the Philippians had any idea that their paths would cross. The apostle first returned to the locations of his initial missionary journey where he added Timothy to his ministry group because he was well spoken of by the brethren (Acts 16:1-3). In visiting the various cities, Paul delivered the Jerusalem Council decrees (16:4-5; cf. Acts 15).

Paul attempted to plough a new field of ministry in Asia and Bithynia, but the Holy Spirit had other plans. So Paul ended up on the eastern Aegean coast in the port city of Troas (16:6-8).

While in Troas, Paul received his unforgettable vision in which he believed God was directing him to preach the gospel in Macedonia. In obedience, the missionary party put out to cross the Aegean Sea, landing at Neapolis near Philippi (16:9-12).

Unlike other major cities where Paul sought out the local synagogue, this Roman colony showed the same hostility towards the Jews as did Rome (18:1-2) and thus no formal synagogue existed. Paul and his party looked outside of the city by the Gangites River (about one mile west of Philippi) for those 'God fearers' who might gather for prayer. There, Lydia turned to Christ for salvation and was baptized along with other members of her household (16:13-15). These new converts constituted the beginnings of the Philippian church— the first church of Europe.

Paul and his group remained to preach the way of salvation which is why God sent them to Philippi. Not surprisingly, overt spiritual warfare erupted during the course of his ministry, in which Paul finally prevailed by breaking up a demon-powered, fortune-telling scam. The owners of the now profitless enterprise, retaliated by bringing charges against Paul and Silas for being Jews in a Roman colony, and inciting religiously inspired opposition to Rome (16:16-20).

Both the public and the chief magistrates reacted with swift punishment by which the two were incarcerated (16:22-24). Who could have guessed that an earthquake would not only quickly release the men from prison, but also result in the second known household believing in Christ for salvation (16:25-34). At least two known houses in Philippi were now devoted to Christ: Lydia's and the Philippian jailer's.

The magistrates soon discovered what a colossal blunder they had made by beating and imprisoning two men with Roman citizenship in a Roman colony. As a result, Paul and Silas were released, enjoyed a time of fellowship with the brethren, and then they took leave of Philippi (16:37-40).

Just how long Paul ministered in Philippi we don't know for sure—probably just weeks (cf. 16:12). There seems to have been more converts than just the two named households. Some have conjectured that Luke remained as pastor until Paul returned on the third missionary journey (20:1-6) about five years later. Luke, however, uses 'us' and 'we' as the party departs Philippi en route to Troas. In all likelihood, Silas later returned to Philippi while Timothy revisited Thessalonica to check up on these two fledgling congregations (17:14-15; 18:5).

The Philippians loved Paul dearly, as evidenced by their ongoing support of his church-planting ministry. They sent gifts more than once while he ministered in Thessalonica (Philippians 4:16). While he laboured in Corinth they also cared for him (4:15). And when Paul was under house arrest in Rome (ca. 61 AD), we discover that they sent Epaphroditus to serve him (cf. 2:19-30; 4:18).

Besides the history of this church as recorded in Acts and Paul's epistle, we have one other solid historical glimpse of the Philippian church. Polycarp wrote a letter to the church about AD 110-120. In this letter, he validates what we already know about the Philippian believers from Scripture.

> These things, brethren, I write unto you concerning right-eousness, not because I laid this charge upon myself, but because ye invited me. For neither am I, nor is any other like unto me, able to follow the wisdom of the blessed and glorious Paul, who when he came among you taught face to face with the men of that day the word which concerneth truth carefully and surely; who also, when he was absent, wrote a letter unto you, into the which if ye look diligently, ye shall be able to be builded up unto the faith given to you, *which is the mother of us all,* while hope followeth after and love goeth before—love toward God and Christ and toward our neighbour. For if any man be occupied with these, he hath fulfilled the commandment of righteousness; for he that hath love is far from all sin.[1]

Commendable Features

The church at Philippi appears to be very much like Philadelphia (Revelation 3:7-13) in that the ministry doors which God had opened stayed open against all odds. God's sovereign hand in this church should encourage us all to look for evidence of the same in our churches today.

Both the historical narration of the church's beginnings in Acts 16:1-40 and Paul's letter written about ten years later provide a tremendous profile of a God-blessed, Christ-centred church worthy of our note. The following discussion highlights the most significant features of the church, all of which can be commended to our churches today.

Evangelistic Fervour

From the beginning of this church, evangelism took centre stage. God re-routed Paul from Asia to Europe to preach the gospel. Finding no Jewish synagogue, Paul sought out 'God-fearing' Gentiles with whom to share Christ. When Paul encountered Lydia, he shared the gospel with her, for it says, 'The Lord opened her heart to respond to the things spoken by Paul' (Acts 16:14). She then submitted to believer's baptism (16:15).

Their ministry later took on an unwanted high profile. The demons cried out, 'These men are bondservants of the Most High God, who are proclaiming to you the way of salvation' (16:17). As a result of the demons being cast out and an economically-inspired, fortune-telling scam being ruined, Paul and Silas landed in prison.

While imprisoned, Paul and Silas prayed and sang hymns of praise to God. It seems their worship took on a public proclamation of the gospel behind bars because 'the prisoners were listening to them' (16:25). Then came the earthquake.

We don't have all of the details, but it would seem likely that the Philippian jailor had heard Paul and Silas preach the gospel prior to his famous question. It was a combination of the earthquake, the thought that he must kill himself and then relief that none of the prisoners had escaped, which prompted the jailer to inquire, 'Sirs, what must I do to be saved?' That well known gospel message then came forth from Paul's lips, 'Believe in the Lord Jesus, and you shall be saved' (16:30-31).

The 'brethren' with whom Paul fellowshipped before his departure to Thessalonica had all been saved during Paul's brief stay at Philippi. Some of them might have been prisoners. Undoubtedly, Paul's example in evangelism spread throughout the congregation. Thus, ten years later Paul wrote his epistle to a healthy, vibrant church which still had a strong gospel witness (Philippians 1:5).

Commentators typically describe Philippians as a book about 'joy' as there are at least thirteen references to this in the epistle. However, few mention the intense concentration on the 'gospel', which is more than any other New Testament book except Romans (cf. 1:5, 7, 12, 16, 27; 2:22; 4:3, 15). The Philippians had not minimized or deprioritized the importance of preaching Christ.

Baptismal Emphasis

One cannot help but be struck with how promptly baptism is mentioned following the conversion of Lydia and the Philippian jailor. It would appear from the narration in Acts 16:13-15 that both Lydia and her household believed and were immediately baptized in the river by which they had gathered that very day.

In the case of the jailer and his family, there can be no doubt about the time sequence of their baptism in relationship to salvation. 'Immediately he was baptized, he and all his household' (16:33). It's apparent that Paul took seriously Jesus' command to baptize in the name of the Father and of the Son and of the Holy Spirit (cf. Matthew 28:19).

Strong Teaching

If Paul took seriously the first two portions of the Great Commission (evangelism and baptism), then we are not surprised to see him labour in the third part also, 'teaching them to observe all that I commanded you' (Matthew 28:20).

While we learn little from Acts 16 about Paul's teaching ministry, his letter to the Philippian church tells us much. To be sure, the epistle proves to be enormously practical and life related. But at the same time, it assumes and alludes to a whole range of theological doctrine. For example:

Angelology	Acts 16:16-18
Anthropology	Philippians 3:8, 17-18
Bibliology	Philippians 1:14; 2:16
Christology	Philippians 1:19; 2:5-11
Ecclesiology	Philippians 1:1
Eschatology	Philippians 1:6, 10, 20-21; 2:16; 3:20-21
Hamartiology	Philippians 3:8
Pneumatology	Philippians 2:1
Soteriology	Philippians 2:12-13
Theology Proper	Philippians 3:14; 4:7

Spiritual Leadership

Philippians 1:1 arguably might be the most important short description of the normal leadership pattern in the New Testament church. Paul was not formally teaching a biblical pattern of church leadership but simply recognizing the norm in his opening remarks to the church.

> Paul and Timothy, bondservants of Christ Jesus, to all the saints in Christ Jesus who are in Philippi, including the overseers and deacons.

Note that all believers are called 'saints'. Then among the saints there were some designated 'overseers' and 'deacons'. This corresponds directly to what Paul would write to Timothy in the near future (1 Timothy 3:1-13).

The term 'overseer' is equated elsewhere in Scripture with 'pastor' and 'elder'. All three terms appear together speaking of one office in Acts 20:17, 28. 1 Peter 5:1-2 equates 'elder' and 'shepherd'. *Overseer* describes the pastor's function of leading/feeding and watching/warning. *Elder* refers to the man's spiritual maturity; while *pastor* describes the role to be played in the church as a shepherd would care for the sheep.

Deacon (and by inference deaconess) refers to those people in the church who have a high level of spiritual maturity and a deep desire to serve the Lord, but who have not been God-gifted in the areas of preaching/teaching and leading. Paul describes their qualifications in 1 Timothy 3:8-13. The general sense of how to serve is illustrated in Acts 6:1-6. Deacons come alongside the overseers to facilitate ministry and leadership in the church so that overseers do not have to be deviate from the priorities of prayer and preaching.

'Saints' does not refer to sinless people but to Christians who have been saved and have the hope of sinlessness in eternity. Put another way, every person in the congregation would be included in 'the saints'. Some had matured in their faith to the point that they were also deacons and overseers. The church in Philippi demonstrates the biblical leadership pattern for a New Testament church, then and now.

Prayer

Paul apparently knew that the Philippians put a high priority on prayer. When he needed God's deliverance from both Roman house arrest and distress caused by other Christian preachers (1:15-17), Paul appealed to the Philippians. He confidently wrote, 'For I know that his shall turn out for my deliverance through your prayers ...' (1:19).

Where did the priority of prayer in the church come from? Remember that Lydia, the first convert at Philippi to receive Christ, had regularly gathered with her household for prayer before her conversion. Undoubtedly this dependence on God through prayer became even more important after salvation. So prayer would have been a major part of the church from the beginning.

The example of Paul certainly encouraged them. 'I thank my God in all my remembrance of you, always offering prayer with joy in my every prayer for you all ... ' (1:3-4). They would have wanted to pray like Paul.

Additionally, Paul instructed them on prayer as was his habit with other churches also (cf. 1 Thessalonians 5:17; 1 Timothy 2:1-2).

> Be anxious for nothing, but in everything by prayer and supplication with thanksgiving let your requests be made known to God. And the peace of God, which surpasses all comprehension, shall guard your hearts and your minds in Christ Jesus (4:6-7).

They would have been moved to obey Paul.

Sovereign Dependence

No one at Philippi could question God's sovereignty in the church. The Lord had expressly redirected Paul out of Asia and on to Europe in order to preach the gospel. About Lydia's conversion the Scripture reports, 'The Lord opened her heart to respond to the things spoken by Paul' (Acts 16:14). The timing of the earthquake, plus its dramatic redemptive results in the Philippian jailor's family, the humiliation of the Roman officials and the release of Paul to continue preaching, certainly exceeded anything that could be called coincidental. God's sovereignty had overwhelmingly given birth to the Philippian church.

God had begun a good work in the lives of individual

Philippians with salvation (1:6). So Paul confidently asserted that God would continue to complete that which He first caused. What would be true of individual Christians in the church would also be true of the church as a whole.

They knew that it was God who was at work in them to will and to work for His good pleasure (2:13). The Lord sovereignly spared Epaphroditus' life by His mercy (2:27). Paul had been 'laid hold of' by Christ Jesus (3:12). God would sovereignly supply all of their needs according to His riches (4:19). Ultimately God would sovereignly cause every knee to bow and every tongue to confess Jesus Christ as Lord to the glory of the Father (2:10-11).

So obvious and so dominant was the idea of God's sovereignty in the church that Paul never explains or defends it—he just describes the Christian life with it. He assumes that deity and sovereignty are inseparable attributes of God. Yet, he doesn't underplay the Philippian responsibility. They are to pray (1:19), to work out their salvation (2:12), to beware of false teachers (3:2) and to stand firm (4:1).

Joyful Attitude
Thirteen times in Philippians Paul refers to joy or rejoicing. The references are split between Paul (1:4,18; 2:2, 17; 4:1, 10) and the Philippians (1:25; 2:18, 28, 29; 3:1; 4:4).

The emphasis of this joy rested in an attitude of rejoicing, regardless of the circumstances. They were to rejoice always, whether in receiving Epaphroditus home alive (2:29) or in suffering for the gospel (2:17-18).

Generosity
From the beginning, the Philippian church practised 'grace giving'. Immediately upon conversion, both Lydia (Acts

16:15) and the Philippian jailer (Acts 16:34) opened up their houses to Paul and his companions.

When Paul departed to Thessalonica, on more than one occasion they provided for his needs (4:15-16). Later in Corinth, the Philippians again cared for Paul (2 Corinthians 11:9). With Paul under house arrest in Rome, ten years after the church began, they still cared for him.

Not only had they sent provisions (4:10, 14, 18) but also a personal helper—Epaphroditus (2:25-30). Undoubtedly when Paul had taken a collection for the suffering church of Jerusalem, the Philippians were one of several Macedonian churches to give abundantly towards the need (see 2 Corinthians 8:1-5).

Jesus once instructed the disciples, 'Freely you received, freely give' (Matthew 10:8). The Philippians contributed sacrificially in that same spirit .

Potential Problems

Unlike Jesus' letters to Ephesus, Pergamum, Thyatira, Sardis and Laodicea, Paul does not condemn the Philippians for anything. However, much like his first letter to Thessalonica, Paul hints that there might be some forthcoming trouble if steps are not taken now towards remedy.

Compromise

Paul devotes much of Philippians 3 to retelling his own conversion from false religion to the true gospel (3:1-16). Very possibly Judaizing messengers had come to Philippi (maybe from Thessalonica). These false teachers tried to divert Christians away from God's grace and back to the Mosaic law as the way of maintaining their salvation.

Then he warns against libertines whose priorities are earthly and fleshly (3:17-21). Whether this is purely preventative or a little more we don't know for certain. But Paul's message comes across clearly—keep pressing on and looking up for the Saviour's return (3:14-16, 20-21).

Disunity

Paul devotes two sections of his letter to unity (1:27-2:11; 4:2-3). The first sounds like a warning over what could happen if they were not careful to cultivate and keep the unity that they already enjoyed. Yet the length of the exhortation makes one wonder if there might not be more emerging disunity than the letter indicates.

However, no one can question the real rift between Euodia and Syntyche (4:2-3). Here Paul appeals to their joint labours on behalf of the gospel as the basis for their reconciliation.

A Caring Church

The Philippian church might best be characterized overall as a 'caring' church. It's obvious that the believers cared lovingly and sacrificially for Paul and his ongoing ministry. They gave like few, if any, other churches. Their gifts extended even to the giving of people like Epaphroditus.

They cared much about the preaching of the gospel and the salvation of unbelievers. The prominent theme of 'the gospel' in Philippians, coupled with Luke's account of the church's beginning in Acts, confirms this. The church had a big heart for evangelism.

Whether Paul urged them to continue caring for one another as they were doing or exhorted them to correct a deficiency in this important area, it is obvious that the believers cared for each other.

11

**CORINTH
THE ADOLESCENT CHURCH**

And I, brethren, could not speak to you as to spiritual men, but as to men of flesh, as to babes in Christ. I gave you milk to drink, not solid food; for you were not yet able to receive it. Indeed, even now you are not yet able, for you are still fleshly. For since there is jealousy and strife among you, are you not fleshly, and are you not walking like mere men? For when one says, 'I am of Paul,' and another, 'I am of Apollos,' are you not mere men? What then is Apollos? And what is Paul? Servants through whom you believed, even as the Lord gave opportunity to each one. I planted, Apollos watered, but God was causing the growth. So then neither the one who plants nor the one who waters is anything, but God who causes the growth. Now he who plants and he who waters are one; but each will receive his own reward according to his own labour. For we are God's fellow workers; you are God's field, God's building (1 Corinthians 3:1-9).

Nowhere in the New Testament does such a wide variety of deviation from the church's biblical blueprint appear in as much detail as in the Corinthian correspondence. The church in Corinth had so much promise and potential at the beginning, but instead of the church's light dispelling the city's spiritual darkness, it was the culture and characteristics of the city that penetrated the church .

Like an adolescent who struggles hard to escape childhood and concurrently stumbles awkwardly towards adulthood, the Corinthian church seemed continually to trip over itself, having more embarrassing moments than commendable ones (1 Corinthians 3:1-3; 2 Corinthians 6:13). While not as spiritually mature as the churches at Ephesus, Pergamum and Thyatira, which were themselves soundly rebuked by Christ, neither had the Corinthian church deteriorated as far as Sardis and Laodicea of whom Christ had nothing good to say.

The City of Corinth

Following the pattern of taking the gospel to the most strategically located cities—like Jerusalem, Antioch, Ephesus, Thessalonica and Philippi—to achieve the fastest, widest spread of the gospel to the largest populations, taking the gospel to the city of Corinth proved to be no exception. A population that might have exceeded 500,000 people set Corinth apart as one of the most populous cities in these studies.

The city of Corinth invited commerce. It served as the hub for both north-south and east-west trade. This city of two seas (Adriatic and Aegean) lay between two major seaports on an isthmus barely four miles across. By transporting goods across the Corinthian isthmus between the ports of Lechaem and Cenchrea, over 200 miles of a dangerous sea voyage could be eliminated. Both national and international commerce had little choice but to pass through Corinth.

The Corinth of Paul's day had been built by Rome about one hundred years earlier (ca. 46 BC). She became the capital for the Roman province of Achaia. Some have suggested that cosmopolitan Corinth resembled the Roman empire in miniature.

Religious pluralism marked Corinth, as might have been expected. Poseidon, the god of the sea, was honoured at the biannual Isthmic games. Aphrodite, the goddess of sexual love, was sensually worshipped atop the Acrocorinth (ca. 1857 feet above the city). Worship of Isis from Egypt, the Great Mother from Phrygia and Dionysus from Thrace were all a part of the religious landscape. Ruins of the temple to Apollo can still be seen there today. The Jews also had their synagogue (Acts 18:4).

The name 'Corinth' had become like 'Sodom and Gomorrah'—associated with sexual sin. To 'Corinthianize' meant to fornicate. A 'Corinthian girl' was a harlot. Along with its wealth and religious diversity came the predictable notoriety of being an openly immoral city known for its debauchery and riotous living.

We are not totally surprised then when we read that the Lord had to encourage Paul in Corinth.

And the Lord said to Paul in the night by a vision, 'Do not be afraid any longer, but go on speaking and do not be silent; for I am with you, and no man will attack you in order to harm you, for I have many people in this city.' And he settled there a year and six months, teaching the word of God among them (Acts 18:9-11).

The Church in Corinth

Paul founded the church during his second missionary journey (ca. AD 51-52). Having departed from Athens, he journeyed about forty miles south to Corinth. There he met up with fellow tent-makers Aquila and Priscilla who had recently been evicted from Rome by Claudius. As was his usual practice, Paul sought to teach in the synagogue every Sabbath, testifying that Jesus was the Christ (Acts 18:1-5).

After Timothy and Silas rejoined Paul, he left the synagogue and reached out to the Gentiles. A few converts are named, such as Titius Justus, who lived next door to the synagogue, and Crispus, the synagogue leader. Sosthenes, who apparently succeeded Crispus as leader of the synagogue, was also converted (see 1 Corinthians 1:1). Paul remained for eighteen months teaching the word of God among them before departing to conclude his second journey by returning to Antioch (Acts 18:5-22).

The church would initially have been comprised of all new converts. Some had come from a sympathetic religious background of Judaism, while others were saved out of the deepest and darkest expressions of idolatry. Most likely, the Gentile converts outnumbered the Jews. With regard to social class, both rich and poor would have been in the church.

Paul later wrote two canonical letters to Corinth. About four years after Paul's arrival (ca. AD 55-56), he wrote 1 Corinthians from Ephesus (Acts 19; 1 Corinthians 16:8) on his third missionary journey, probably in response to reports from Chloe's people (1:11) plus the information received from Stephanas, Fortunatus and Achaicus (16:17). Months later he penned 2 Corinthians from Macedonia (Acts 20; 2 Corinthians 7:5). From these two letters we will glean both the commendable and condemnable features of the Corinthian church.

Commendable Features

Spiritual Potential

The Corinthian church lacked no spiritual grace in order for her to flourish with the best of churches like Antioch or Philadelphia. The believers had been enriched in all speech and knowledge (1 Corinthians 1:5); they lacked no gift for ministry (1:7); they had been sanctified in Christ Jesus (1:2) and called into fellowship with Him, God's own Son.

Prayer

Apparently Paul knew of the Corinthians' prayer for him (2 Corinthians 1:11). So he commends the Corinthians for those petitions which would be rendered on his behalf.

Standing Firm

'For in your faith you are standing firm' (2 Corinthians 1:24). This might sound strange in light of the Corinthians' reputation, so we ask, 'What faith?'

Earlier Paul had commended them for continuing to stand in the gospel faith that he delivered to Corinth:

> Now I make known to you, brethren, the gospel which I preached to you, which also you received, in which also you stand (1 Corinthians 15:1).

Even though they deviated and disobeyed on many fronts, the gospel was not one of them.

Holding to Sound Doctrine

The Corinthians remembered what Paul had taught them and held firmly to the tradition, that is, the doctrine which he had taught (1 Corinthians 11:2). They had not compromised their doctrinal statement in terms of personal belief.

Condemnable Features

While all of these commendable features would certainly have met with Christ's approval, the overwhelming quality of the church in general deserved the Saviour's rebuke. The following condemnable characteristics comprise the far larger portion of commentary on the Corinthian church.

Arrogant Divisions

The Corinthians had quickly identified with men rather than God (1 Corinthians 11:18-19). Some were of Paul, others Apollos, and still others Cephas (1 Corinthians 1:12). This mindset in the church divided rather than unified. This unholy emphasis spilled over to tarnish the normally bright joy of baptism (1 Corinthians 1:13-17).

Paul turns them back to being God-centred rather than man-centred (1 Corinthians 3:21-23). He portrays himself and his ministry partners as servants of Christ (1 Corinthians 4:1) and reminds them of their undeserved call to salvation (1 Corinthians 1:26-31). Paul calls the Corinthians back to humble unity.

> Now I exhort you, brethren, by the name of our Lord Jesus Christ, that you all agree, and there be no divisions among you, but you be made complete in the same mind and in the same judgment (1 Corinthians 1:10).

Prolonged Spiritual Immaturity

Paul had to speak to them like children (2 Corinthians 6:13), as though they were babes in Christ, that is, new believers (1

Corinthians 3:1). Jealousy and strife characterized the church (1 Corinthians 3:3).

They should have been able to receive solid food, spiritually speaking, but instead Paul had to deliver milk, as to a babe (1 Corinthians 3:2). They were more concerned about their own petty allegiances than in exalting Christ and acknowledging God as the One who causes the church to grow (1 Corinthians 3:4-9).

Toleration of Sin

Like the church at Thyatira, Corinth allowed sin to fester within the church (1 Corinthians 5:1-2). The nature of this sin exceeded the vilest activities that even an unbelieving Corinthian would tolerate (1 Corinthian 5:1). Paul called for the Corinthians to remove the unrepentant sinner from the assembly (1 Corinthians 5:13).

Sueing One Another

Apparently believers were initiating lawsuits in the secular courts against other believers (1 Corinthian 6:1, 6). Paul calls for an end to this and reasons that it would be better to lose than to win the wrong way (1 Corinthians 6:7).

Immorality

While Paul does not come right out with a direct accusation, it would appear that he at least had suspicions that some Corinthian Christians were engaged in the kind of immorality for which the city was so well known (1 Corinthians 6:15-20). He warns them to 'Flee immorality' (1 Corinthians 6:18). And in 1 Corinthians 6:20, 'For you have been bought with a price; therefore glorify God in your body' comprises Paul's closing words on this subject.

Abusing Christian Liberty

Paul spends three chapters (1 Corinthians 8-10) dealing with this issue which arose in the context of eating meat previously sacrificed to idols (1 Corinthians 8:1; 10:14-22).

In order to solve the problem that converted Jews would have with Gentiles who felt free to buy meat previously offered to idols, Paul offers two pieces of advice:

> All things are lawful, but not all things are profitable. All things are lawful, but not all things edify. Let no one seek his own good, but that of his neighbour (1 Corinthians 10:23-24).

> Whether, then, you eat or drink or whatever you do, do all to the glory of God (1 Corinthians 10:31).

Profaning the Lord's Supper

What should have been most sacred turned out instead to be most profaned. Divisions plus gluttony and drunkenness characterized their love feasts and celebrations of the Lord's Supper. Paul accuses them of despising the church by such behaviour (1 Corinthians 11:18-22).

The unholy is to be corrected by a return to the holy. Paul reminds them of what he had received directly from Christ (1 Corinthians 11:23-26). If they fail to repent, then sickness or even death awaits them as God's judgment (1 Corinthians 11:29-30).

Misappropriation of Spiritual Gifts

Every believer, without exception, had been given outworkings of the Holy Spirit for the common good (1 Corinthians 12:7). In their zeal, the Corinthians had sought out gifts according to their desires and not the Lord's (1 Corinthians 12:12-30).

Further, the Corinthians exercised their giftedness for self-edification rather than edification of the church (1 Corinthians 14:12).

Paul points them back to love as the attitude in which spiritual gifts are to be ministered (1 Corinthians 13:1-13). Order and proper exercising of gifts, not confusion, are to be the outcome (2 Corinthians 14:33, 40).

Failure to Correct False Doctrine
Some in the church were saying, 'There is no resurrection of the dead' (1 Corinthians 15:12). Paul provides the most detailed biblical defence of the resurrection in response (1 Corinthians 15:12-58).

Apparently it was only a handful of people who embraced this major doctrinal error. Paul had earlier commended the church for standing firm on the gospel (1 Corinthians 15:1). His comment should be seen not so much as a rebuke as the correction of bad doctrine with true teaching.

Unwilling to Forgive
Whether this refers back to 1 Corinthians 5 or not, we are unable to tell for sure. However, it is apparent that someone in the church had sinned and repented, but the church was unwilling to forgive (2 Corinthians 2:8-11). Paul exhorts them to follow his apostolic lead and forgive (verse 10). In so doing they will avoid being duped by Satan into continuing their refusal to forgive true repentance (verse 11).

Slow to Give
A glimmer of this problem might be detected in Paul's first letter (1 Corinthians 16:1-9). By the time of 2 Corinthians, this had become a major source of embarrassment (2 Corin-

thians 8-9). The poorer brethren of Macedonia had already fulfilled their promise to give for the impoverished church in Jerusalem (2 Corinthians 8:1-2). In contrast the wealthier church at Corinth had failed to deliver that which was promised (2 Corinthians 9:1-5).

Critical of Spiritual Leadership

It is apparent throughout 2 Corinthians that the church has been openly hostile towards Paul. The situation is most explicitly discussed in 2 Corinthians 10-12. This is the most strained relationship we know of between Paul and any of the churches to whom he ministered.

Paul summarized the situation by saying that if anyone should be put to the test, it ought to be the Corinthians, not the apostle.

> Test yourselves to see if you are in the faith; examine yourselves! Or do you not recognize this about yourselves, that Jesus Christ is in you—unless indeed you fail the test? But I trust that you will realize that we ourselves do not fail the test (2 Corinthians 13:5-6).

A Final Word

Human wisdom—mixed liberally with pride rather than humility—to the exclusion of God's wisdom not only resists the work of God in a believer's life, but also invites Satan to take undue advantage of the believer (2 Corinthians 2:11). Such was the sad situation at Corinth.

Paul's two letters to Corinth speak of Satan's activities more than the writings to any other single church (cf. 1 Corinthians 5:5; 7:5; 10:20-21; 2 Corinthians 2:11; 4:4; 11:3; 11:14). He expresses his love and shepherd's heart for the Corinthians in this manner:

> But I am afraid, lest as the serpent deceived Eve by his craftiness, your minds should be led astray from the simplicity and purity of devotion to Christ (2 Corinthians 11:3).

Paul knew that the believers in Corinth were not ignorant of Satan's schemes or mindgames (2 Corinthians 2:11). Apparently, they had ignored the warnings of Scripture and consequently were outwitted by the enemy. You have the same information and need to remember that the devil, not Christ, would like your church to look like the Corinthian assembly with the following condemnable features:

1. Arrogant divisions.
2. Prolonged spiritual immaturity.
3. Toleration of sin.
4. Sueing one another.
5. Immorality.
6. Abusing Christian liberty.
7. Profaning the Lord's Supper.
8. Misappropriation of spiritual gifts.
9. Failure to correct false doctrine.
10. Unwilling or slow to forgive.
11. Critical of spiritual leadership.

This is the profile of a church whose collective mind had been deceived by Satan and led astray from the simplicity and purity of devotion to Christ. Be warned and beware! This is what the church looks like when the devil, not Christ, is her head.

If the church had heeded Paul's instructions on love in 1 Corinthians 13:4-7, imagine what a difference there would be. Here is the personal profile of a church that loves:

1. 'Love is patient.' Therefore, I will bear with *another's* worst behaviour, without retaliation, regardless of the circumstances.

2. 'Love is kind.' Therefore, I will diligently seek ways to be actively useful in *another's* life.

3. 'Love is not jealous.' Therefore, I will delight in the esteem and honour given to *another*.

4. 'Love does not brag.' Therefore, I will not draw attention to myself exclusive of *someone else*.

5. 'Love is not arrogant.' Therefore, I know I am not more important than *someone else*.

6. 'Love does not act unbecomingly.' Therefore, I will not engage *another* in ungodly activity.

7. 'Love does not seek its own.' Therefore, I will be *one-another* oriented.

8. 'Love is not provoked.' Therefore, I will not resort to anger as a solution to difficulties between myself and *someone else*.

9. 'Love does not take into account a wrong suffered.' Therefore, I will never keep an account due on *someone else*.

10. 'Love does not rejoice in unrighteousness.' Therefore, I will never delight in *another's* unrighteous behaviour, nor will I join in its expression.

11. 'Love rejoices with the truth.' Therefore, I will find great joy when truth prevails in *another's* life.

12. 'Love bears all things.' Therefore, I will be publicly silent about *another's* faults.

13. 'Love believes all things.' Therefore, I will express unshakable confidence and trust in *someone else*.

14. 'Love hopes all things.' Therefore, I will confidently expect future victory in *another's* life, regardless of the present imperfections.

15. 'Love endures all things.' Therefore, I will outlast every assault of Satan to break up my relationship with *someone else*.

PART THREE

THE CHURCHES OF THE EAST

12

ANTIOCH
THE SENDING CHURCH

Now there were at Antioch, in the church that was there, prophets and teachers: Barnabas, and Simeon who was called Niger, and Lucius of Cyrene, and Manaen who had been brought up with Herod the tetrarch, and Saul. And while they were ministering to the Lord and fasting, the Holy Spirit said, 'Set apart for Me Barnabas and Saul for the work to which I called them.' Then, when they had fasted and prayed and laid their hands on them, they sent them away. So, being sent out by the Holy Spirit, they went down to Seleucia and from there they sailed to Cyprus (Acts 13:1-4).

In this chapter, Scripture references are from the Book of Acts unless otherwise specified.

Our sparse knowledge of early church life at Antioch stands in direct disproportion to the city's size and to her significance in spreading the gospel. During the time period in Acts 11-13 (ca. AD 45-50), Antioch had a population believed to be about 500,000 people; only Rome and Alexandria exceeded her importance to the Roman Empire.

Ancient Antioch (modern Antakya) lay 300 miles north of Jerusalem. Seleucia Pieria served as Antioch's seaport, with Antioch being fifteen miles inland on the navigable Orontes River. Sixteen cities were named Antioch in ancient days, this Antioch had been named by Selecus I (ca. 300 BC) in honour of his father, Antiochus. To aid identification, the city was designated 'Antioch on the Orontes.'

Built at the foot of Mount Sylphus, Antioch stood as the provincial capital of Syria. This celebrated city was well known as a prominent centre of Hellenistic culture and generally recognized as one of the showplaces of the ancient world.

Religiously, the groves of Daphne and the sanctuary of Apollo represented Antioch's idolatry. These centres of pagan worship, located about five miles outside of Antioch, achieved notoriety for cultic prostitution. Thus, Antioch deserved her title 'The Heathen Queen'. Economically, Antioch occupied a prominent location on the main route for east-west commercial traffic.

Cosmopolitan Antioch uniquely qualified to be the launching point for the gospel into Asia and Europe. Biblically, Antioch first appears in Acts 6 with regard to Nicolas who came to Jerusalem from Antioch. With the scattering of the church about AD 35 as a result of Stephen's stoning (Acts 8:1), many believers made their way to Antioch (Acts 11:19).

Luke makes it crystal clear that the gospel reached Antioch

in two distinct segments. First, the Jews, who historically had a large population in Antioch, were reached by those who came from Jerusalem. A second group came from Cyprus and Cyrene with a primary ministry to Gentiles. The Lord blessed this witness to Christ and a large number of people believed (Acts 11:19-21). Apparently, little friction existed between Jewish believers and Gentile believers, except for the issue over the Mosaic law that prompted the Jerusalem Council about 49 AD (cf. Acts 15:1-2; Galatians 2:11-14).

The Christian remnant at Jerusalem heard of God's initial work in Antioch and dispatched Barnabas. Acting in character, Barnabas encouraged the church so that it flourished, with considerable numbers being brought to the Lord (Acts 11:22-24).

Barnabas later located Paul in Tarsus and brought him to Antioch where they taught together for an entire year (Acts 11:25-26). After carrying a special love offering from Antioch to Jerusalem, Paul and Barnabas returned with John Mark (11:27-30; 12:25).

This brief, biblical summary of the church beginnings at Antioch (ca. AD 35-48) sets the stage for Paul's subsequent missionary journeys, all of which originated from Antioch. What we can know for sure about the church itself remains sketchy, but much help can be gleaned from the 'bare bones' account in Acts. Here we explore the major observable features.

Boldness
Believers in Jesus were first called Christians in Antioch (Acts 11:26). Literally, they were of 'the party of Jesus'. This new title made a clear distinction between the Jews of the city and those who put their faith in Christ.

It's not certain whether the church or the community originated the title 'Christian'. However, the church seems to have accepted it as a name that clearly identified their spiritual allegiance (cf. 1 Peter 4:16). 'Christian' quickly became the accepted designation of believers, even to the point that Agrippa told Paul, 'In a short time you will persuade me to become a Christian' (Acts 26:28).

Jewish opposition to Christianity did not seem to be as intense in Antioch as in Jerusalem and Thessalonica. However, the church boldly took the name *Christian* which publicly and unmistakably declared to everyone in the city that they believed in and followed Jesus Christ. In contrast to Joseph of Arimathea, who earlier in Jerusalem had chosen to be a secret believer for fear of the Jews (John 19:38), the believers at Antioch made full public disclosure of their spiritual persuasion.

Growth

On three occasions, Luke comments on the unusual vitality of the ministry at Antioch.

> And the hand of the Lord was with them, and a large number who believed turned to the Lord (Acts 11:21).

> And considerable numbers were brought to the Lord (Acts 11:24).

> But the word of the Lord continued to grow and to be multiplied (Acts 12:24).

The church grew at an explosive rate because God blessed the true preaching of the gospel.

Antioch provides a classic illustration of a church that grew almost exclusively through the effort of evangelism.

The believers clearly assumed that the gospel represented God's power to save people from their sins.

Ministry Of The Holy Spirit

It is clear that the spiritual leadership at Antioch depended upon God's Spirit as their power for ministry. Barnabas, the spiritual leader dispatched to Antioch from Jerusalem, is described as a man who was full of or totally controlled by the Holy Spirit. As a result, considerable numbers were brought to the Lord (Acts 11:24). Agabus prophesied by the Holy Spirit (Acts 11:28), and, more specifically, the Holy Spirit directed that Paul and Barnabas be dispatched on the first missionary journey. They were sovereignly sent out by the Holy Spirit (Acts 13:2-4).

Godly Leadership

Barnabas was a man with three distinctive characteristics: (1) a good man, (2) full of the Holy Spirit, and (3) full of faith (Acts 11:24). His initial ministry in Antioch took the form of encouraging the believers to remain true to the Lord (11:23).

Paul arrived in Antioch by invitation of Barnabas and for one entire year they taught the church (11:25-26). These two, in evidence of their godliness and undaunted commitment, were set apart by the Holy Spirit for the uniquely significant first missionary journey. In the spirit of Isaiah, who lived hundreds of years before, they not only led the church but led the spread of the gospel to where it had not yet been heard (Isaiah 6:5-13).

Commitment To Preaching And Teaching

When the men from Cyprus and Cyrene arrived in Antioch they preached the Lord Jesus (Acts 11:20). When the scattered Jerusalem believers arrived they came speaking God's Word (11:19).

Then Barnabas and Paul arrived to teach God's Word to the new believers for one year (11:26). The church at Antioch had both prophets and teachers (13:1). The Word of God, whether preached or taught, stood central to the life of the church.

When Paul and Barnabas were sent from Antioch on the first missionary journey, they continued to do elsewhere what they had been doing in Antioch. They proclaimed the Word of God (13:5). In fact, Acts 13 tells us that an entire city assembled to hear the Word of God (verse 44). Consequently, the Word of the Lord spread through the whole region (verse 49).

Returning to Antioch after the Jerusalem Council, Paul and Barnabas picked up where they had left off. 'But Paul and Barnabas stayed in Antioch, teaching and preaching, with many others also, the Word of the Lord' (15:35).

Discipleship
Two passages stand out in reflecting this reality at Antioch.

> ... and when he had found him, he brought him to Antioch. And it came about that for an entire year they met with the church, and taught considerable numbers; and the disciples were first called Christians in Antioch (Acts 11:26).

> And they spent a long time with the disciples (Acts 14:28).

'Disciples' and 'discipleship' dominate the pages of the Gospels and Acts with over 250 mentions. The words refer to a learner/mentor relationship. To become a Christian is to become a learner who sits at the feet of a new found Master— Jesus Christ. 'Take My yoke upon you, and learn from Me' has become one of the most memorable of Christ's invitations to eternal life (Matthew 11:29).

In the Book of Acts, where Luke focuses on believers and their activities, every time the discipleship concept appears (29 times), with one exception, it refers to a Christian. There is no distinction between being a believer now and a disciple later. All the members of the church are referred to as disciples (Acts 6:2, 7; 15:10; 18:23). Acts 26:28 compared with Acts 11:26 equates being a Christian with being a disciple (see also 9:26; 20:30).

One becomes a disciple by responding to God's gospel of grace (Acts 14:21; 18:27). There are no instances of a 'non-disciple' believer. One writer summarizes his conclusions about the learner/master relationship with Jesus in an unforgettable way.

> The disciple of Jesus is not the deluxe or heavy-duty model of the Christian—specially padded, textured, streamlined and empowered for the fast lane on the straight and narrow. He stands on the pages of the New Testament as the first level of basic transportation in the kingdom of God.[1]

Generosity

As Jerusalem had sent its best in the person of Barnabas, whom the new church at Antioch needed for spiritual bolstering, so Antioch later had an opportunity to return the favour.

Famine had further affected the already economically beleaguered church in Jerusalem, so a collection was taken for the 'first' church. Antioch gave to others of the household of faith, that is, the brethren (Acts 11:27-29).

Interestingly, everyone of the Christians at Antioch contributed (11:29-30). Not everyone gave the same amount, but in proportion to their financial situation. It could well have been that the church at Antioch knew of Barnabas' own example during the very early days in the Jerusalem church when generosity abounded.

> And Joseph, a Levite of Cyprian birth, who was also called Barnabas by the apostles (which translated means, Son of Encouragement), and who owned a tract of land, sold it and brought the money and laid it at the apostles' feet (Acts 4:36-37).

Outreach

Apart from Jerusalem, no church in Scripture has been as intimately connected with the spread of the gospel as Antioch. Acts 13:1-4 provides a tantalizing glimpse of the sending process that resulted in the gospel eventually reaching the world's capital—Rome.

Everyone wishes Luke had given more details to answer our practical 'how to' questions. But he did include enough details to establish some basic, timeless principles.

First, the departure of Paul and Barnabas was initiated by the Holy Spirit. The first missionary journey conformed to the call and will of God, not man.

Second, the church submitted to God and committed these two to advance the gospel beyond Antioch. They were sent both by the Holy Spirit and by the church.

Third, the church willingly gave their best men—Paul and Barnabas—in obedience to the Lord's direction.

Fourth, the call to go came in the midst of first being faithful to ministry at home.

Fifth, the church allowed the outreach process to continue, in that neither Paul nor Barnabas ever returned to Antioch permanently. The church did not try selfishly to keep them at home.

Sixth, a significant level of accountability marked the process. They went out in teams rather than by themselves, for example, Paul, Barnabas and John Mark (Acts 13:5); Paul, Silas and Timothy (Acts 15:40-16:3); or Barnabas and John Mark (Acts 15:39). At the conclusion of their journeys, they returned home to report what had transpired (Acts 14:26-28; 18:22-23).

Doctrinal Discernment

While Paul and Barnabas spent time with the church after their first missionary journey, some men from Jerusalem came teaching that circumcision was required for salvation. Apparently unable to resolve this issue of great doctrinal and practical importance, the church dispatched Paul and Barnabas to Jerusalem (Acts 15:1-2).

Highlights of the Jerusalem conference report that the discernment of Antioch prevailed (15:3-21). A clarifying letter was written both to Antioch plus to Syria and Cilicia (15:23-29). At its reading the church was encouraged (15:30-31).

The Christians rejoiced not that they prevailed personally or as a church, but rather that the truth prevailed and the heresy of a 'salvation by circumcision' had been repudiated as false doctrine. Antioch's doctrinal discernment saved the church immeasurable grief from trouble which certainly would have come later if the issue had not been dealt with decisively here.

A Basic Sketch

You can try to read between the lines for more details, but the church at Antioch displayed the following noteworthy qualities for sure:

- Boldness
- Growth
- Ministry of the Holy Spirit
- Godly leadership
- Commitment to preaching and teaching
- Discipleship
- Generosity
- Outreach
- Doctrinal discernment

13

JERUSALEM
THE FIRST CHURCH

And with many other words he solemnly testified and kept on exhorting them, saying, 'Be saved from this perverse generation!' So then, those who had received his word were baptized; and there were added that day about three thousand souls. And they were continually devoting themselves to the apostles' teaching and to fellowship, to the breaking of bread and to prayer. And everyone kept feeling a sense of awe; and many wonders and signs were taking place through the apostles. And all those who had believed were together, and had all things in common; and they began selling their property and possessions, and were sharing them with all, as anyone might have need. And day by day continuing with one mind in the temple, and house, they were taking their meals together with gladness and sincerity of heart, praising God, and having favour with all the people. And the Lord was adding to their number day by day those who were being saved (Acts 2:40-47).

In this chapter, Scripture references are from the Book of Acts unless otherwise specified.

When you look around in almost any American city or town, you will be certain to find 'The First Church of _____.' While it might be the first church of its kind in that location, there can be only one genuine 'first' church. The Jerusalem church authentically claims the unique title of 'The First Church'.

By virtue of its absolute 'newness', the Jerusalem church provides the best portrait of what Christ designed the church to be. Human beings had not yet had time or opportunity to desecrate her. Just as Eden had a pristine quality before Satan deceived Eve and sin marred its beauty (Genesis 3:1-7), so the Jerusalem assembly had an unequalled spiritual wholesomeness before Satan deceived Ananias and Sapphira, which then opened the gateway for sin to flood into the church (Acts 5:1-11).

Jerusalem represents the prototype for all subsequent churches. The effect of salvation was fresh for everyone; the work of the Holy Spirit in salvation was powerful; and the desire of the congregation to glorify God in every aspect of their lives set the standard for all future churches to follow. Even more so than Smyrna, Philadelphia, Thessalonica and Philippi, the Jerusalem church in its beginnings portrayed most clearly what God intended the church to be and to do.

The following exposition allows us to look at the major highlights of this model church. Everything we see at Jerusalem in principle will be applicable to your church today. For pastors and those who like to be theologically minded, let me suggest that a study of this church is the best of 'applied ecclesiology'.

A High View of Scripture
As one reads the book of Acts, it quickly becomes evident that the church acknowledged only one source of authority for ministry—the Scriptures. Whether it was preaching

evangelistically, teaching doctrine, rebuking religious leaders, responding to government officials, or deciding matters within the church, the Scripture took centre stage as the only basis for their message or decisions.

Twice, Luke specifically mentions the overall effect of God's Word on the ministry: 'And the word of God kept on spreading' (Acts 6:7); 'But the word of the Lord continued to grow and to be multiplied' (Acts 12:24). The truth of Isaiah's great passage on Scripture was being lived out in Jerusalem:

> 'For My thoughts are not your thoughts, neither are your ways My ways,' declares the LORD. 'For as the heavens are higher than the earth, so are My ways higher than your ways, and My thoughts than your thoughts. For as the rain and the snow come down from heaven, and do not return there without watering the earth, and making it bear and sprout, and furnishing seed to the sower and bread to the eater; so shall My word be which goes forth from My mouth; it shall not return to Me empty, without accomplishing what I desire, and without succeeding in the matter for which I sent it' (Isaiah 55:8-11).

Look at Peter's great sermon on Pentecost which actually launched the church (Acts 2:14-40). He quotes lengthy passages from the Psalms and Joel. Most of the remaining portions allude to Scripture. In his second major message, Peter again focuses on Scripture for the authoritative basis and the content of what he preached (3:12-26). The same held true also for the third message (4:8-12).

The church's prayer after the apostles had been released from jail is noteworthy: 'Grant that Thy bondservants may speak Thy word with all confidence' (4:29). Jerusalem can be characterized as wholeheartedly a church of God's Word.

This church lived out what Paul would later write concerning Scripture.

> All Scripture is inspired by God and profitable for teaching, for reproof, for correction, for training in righteousness; that the man of God may be adequate, equipped for every good work (2 Timothy 3:16-17).

Reliance On The Holy Spirit

The Holy Spirit inaugurated the church at Jerusalem. Jesus had told the disciples that they would be baptized with the Holy Spirit not many days after He ascended to heaven (Acts 1:5). Further, He instructed them:

> '... but you shall receive power when the Holy Spirit has come upon you; and you shall be My witnesses both in Jerusalem, and in all Judea and Samaria, and even to the remotest part of the earth' (Acts 1:8).

Ten days later the Holy Spirit came upon the disciples, they preached Christ and the church began (Acts 2:1-41). Luke mentions the Holy Spirit over 55 times in Acts, beginning at 1:2 and finishing at 28:25. The Spirit's ministry certainly cannot be limited to Pentecost alone since it continued long after the first days.

Repeatedly, the Acts narrative recounts that the Holy Spirit 'filled' or controlled either individuals or groups of people. The apostles were filled with the Holy Spirit and spoke of the mighty deeds of God (2:4, 11). The Spirit controlled Peter's preaching (4:8). The whole church was filled with the Holy Spirit (4:31). The leadership of the church also needed to be led by the Spirit (6:3, 5).

The church experienced then what Paul would later commend to the Ephesians:

> Therefore be careful how you walk, not as unwise men, but as wise, making the most of your time, because the days are evil. So then do not be foolish, but understand what the will of the Lord is. And do not get drunk with wine, for that is dissipation, but be filled with the Spirit, speaking to one another in psalms and hymns and spiritual songs, singing and making melody with your heart to the Lord; always giving thanks for all things in the name of our Lord Jesus Christ to God, even the Father; and be subject to one another in the fear of Christ (Ephesians 5:15-21).

The Discipline Of Prayer

The church had a deep commitment to prayer even before she officially commenced. In the ten days between Christ's ascension and Pentecost, the 120 disciples, with one mind, continually devoted themselves to prayer (Acts 1:14). The church-to-be expressed its absolute dependence on God in prayers which reflected the true heart of these God-focused people.

As a congregation after Pentecost, they continually devoted themselves to prayer (2:42). The apostolic leadership set the example for prayer, especially Peter and John (3:1).

Particularly noteworthy was the church's response to persecution. When the apostles had been released from prison and returned to the flock, the church prayed (4:23-31). Most likely in answer to specific prayers, the believers began to speak the Word of God with boldness (4:31).

The apostles set out prayer as the first of two primary responsibilities of spiritual leadership (6:4). New leaders were committed to the Lord's service through prayer (6:6).

Prayer could be found everywhere in the life of the Jerusalem church: Stephen prayed before he died (7:60); the church prayed when James and Peter were imprisoned (12:5, 12); their fervent prayer prevailed as Peter miraculously walked out of prison (12:6-11). God's answer to prayer proved so remarkable, that both Peter (12:11) and the church (12:13-16) were stunned at first, before realizing that the Lord had specifically delivered Peter just as they had been praying that He would.

Bold Evangelism

Modern churches normally begin church planting with a group of mature believers. Then they add to themselves other believers who are looking for a new church because they are dissatisfied with their old congregation. It was not so with Jerusalem. The very first message preached called the community to repentance (Acts 2:38-40). Around an extremely small core of relatively new believers was added a sizeable group of brand-new believers.

Everywhere one looked in those early days, the gospel was being preached. When the people gathered around Peter and John because the lame man had been healed, Peter preached Christ crucified and risen (3:11-4:2).

When confronted by the religious leaders over his ministry, Peter again preached Christ (4:5-12). When jailed, the apostles were released by an angel with this mandate, 'Go your way, stand and speak to the people in the temple the whole message of this Life' (5:20). Or in other words, 'Keep preaching the gospel!' As commanded, they continued to preach Christ (5:24-32). And every day, in the temple and from house to house, they kept on teaching and preaching Jesus as the Christ.

Certain individuals stand out as sterling examples of

evangelism: Stephen preached the gospel just before he was stoned to death (7:2-53); Philip evangelized the crowds (8:12) and the Ethiopian eunuch (8:26-39); Peter went to Cornelius and his household (Acts 10-11).

We would note as a corollary that baptism, in obedience to Christ's command (Matthew 28:19), is closely connected as the first act of obedience after salvation. Peter preached baptism (Acts 2:38) and practised it (2:41). Philip baptized both groups (8:12) and individuals (8:38). Paul was baptized (9:18) and Peter baptized Cornelius with his household (10:48).

Church Growth
The Lord wanted all who would read Luke's account of the Jerusalem church to know that, in spite of fierce opposition, the church grew. An amazing litany of statistics is provided to chronicle the progress. Make no mistake about it, the Jerusalem church experienced church growth—God's way—in a sustained manner over a period of about twenty years. This is what Jesus had in mind when He said, 'I will build My church' (Matthew 16:18).

So then, those who had received his word were baptized; and there were added that day about three thousand souls (Acts 2:41).

... And the Lord was adding to their number day by day those who were being saved (Acts 2:47).

But many of those who had heard the message believed; and the number of the men came to be about five thousand (Acts 4:4). And all the more believers in the Lord, multitudes of men and women, were constantly added to their number (Acts 5:14).

And the word of God kept on spreading; and the number of the disciples continued to increase greatly in Jerusalem, and a great many of the priests were becoming obedient to the faith (Acts 6:7).

So the church throughout all Judea and Galilee and Samaria enjoyed peace, being built up; and going on in the fear of the Lord and in the comfort of the Holy Spirit, it continued to increase (Acts 9:31).

And the hand of the Lord was with them, and a large number who believed turned to the Lord ... And considerable numbers were brought to the Lord (Acts 11:21, 24).

But the word of the Lord continued to grow and to be multiplied (Acts 12:24).

A High Standard Of Commitment

'But none of the rest dared to associate with them; however, the people held them in high esteem' (Acts 5:13). Why wouldn't the population associate with the church? Why did the people hold the church in high esteem?

Most likely, the church was held in high esteem because of its convictions and commitment. No amount of persecution could cause the believers to compromise the gospel or their call to proclaim Christ crucified and resurrected. Nor could God's high standard of holiness cause believers to leave the church. These Christians were committed at the highest level, which is always an admirable trait whether one embraces the cause or looks in from the outside (cf. 2:47, 'having favour with all the people').

But, if their esteem ranked so high, why wouldn't people want to associate with the church? The answer is because of the persecution for preaching (4:1-23), those on the outside realized that to become a part of the church would be to invite the same kind of punishment from the religious and governmental officials. And not only would they be subjected to pressure from the outside, but also from the inside.

Ananias and Sapphira had been struck dead by God for deceit (5:1-10) and as a result, great fear came upon all who heard of these things (5:10-11). God's seriousness about holiness in the church could not have been illustrated and reinforced more dramatically. This level of holiness would not be flippantly violated or forgotten for some significant time to come.

The general population must have thought, 'If I join this group, either the government will get me for joining or God will get me when I don't live up to His demanding standards.' Therefore, the people did not dare to associate with the church, even though they held the church in high esteem.

The issue here is that the church as a whole was more concerned about whether God esteemed them rather than what the people thought. To please God, they must preach Christ and probably be persecuted, but must also live holy lives to avoid the possibility of God's swift judgment (1 Peter 4:17).

Willingness To Sacrifice
This trait, perhaps better than all others, measures the level of one's commitment. If the reward for punishment, or even death, more than compensates for the pain and loss, then the highest level of faithfulness and sacrifice will be reached. This was true for the new church because the worst that could have happened (humanly speaking) was death, which would then allow them instantly to be in the presence of Jesus. This courageous mindset takes people to unbelievable heights of willingness to suffer.

Persecution began with the mocking charge of drunkenness (2:13) and quickly escalated. The disciples were eventually imprisoned (4:3); and when told to stop preaching, they replied, 'We cannot stop speaking what we have seen and heard' (4:20).

They were returned to jail for a second time shortly afterwards (5:18). When brought before the officials and ordered once again not to preach, they responded, 'We must obey God not man' (5:29). Then they were beaten and ordered again to preach no more (5:40). Their response is remarkable.

> So they went on their way from the presence of the Council, rejoicing that they had been considered worthy to suffer shame for His name. And every day, in the temple and from house to house, they kept right on teaching and preaching Jesus as the Christ (Acts 5:41-42).

When the officials could stand it no longer, they took the drastic step of making Stephen an example by stoning him to death (7:54-60). Following this, a great persecution arose against the church and the believers were scattered outside of Jerusalem (8:1). The persecution raged so severe that the church was ravaged house by house with the end result being prison for many (8:3).

Persecution did not discourage or quiet the church, however. Just the opposite took place. 'Therefore, those who had been scattered went about preaching the word' (8:4). The greater the level of suffering, the deeper their commitment became and the wider the gospel spread.

A Great Commission Orientation

Before Jesus ascended to heaven, He commanded the disciples,

> ... 'but you shall receive power when the Holy Spirit has come upon you; and you shall be My witnesses both in

Jerusalem, and in all Judea and Samaria, and even to the remotest part of the earth' (Acts 1:8).

The whole of Acts involves the spread of the gospel from Jerusalem (Acts 1) to Rome (Acts 28). It recounts Peter's ministry to the Jews (Acts 1-12) and Paul's to the Gentiles (Acts 13-28).

Christianity did not remain limited to the immediate community of the Jerusalem church. Yet, a great price (humanly speaking) would be paid for this Great Commission commitment. The church was almost destroyed (8:1-3), but God let it rebound.

> So the church throughout all Judea and Galilee and Samaria enjoyed peace, being built up; and, going on in the fear of the Lord and in the comfort of the Holy Spirit, it continued to increase (Acts 9:31).

Meanwhile, the church in Jerusalem and the brethren of Judea had been devastated economically by strong opposition to Christianity. So, churches from other regions where the gospel had spread decided that,

> ... in the proportion that any of the disciples had means, each of them determined to send a contribution for the relief of the brethren living in Judea (Acts 11:29).

Nevertheless, the outward spiral of the gospel from Jerusalem continued unstoppable. It spread throughout Judea and Samaria (8:1, 25, 40). The eunuch would take the gospel to Ethiopia (8:26-39). It had reached Damascus (9:2), Phoenicia (11:19), Cyprus (11:19), Antioch (11:20) and the Gentiles of Caesarea (chapters 10-11). Shortly, it would spread to Asia, then Europe, and ultimately to the capital of the Roman Empire (28:14).

Well Defined Priorities

From its beginning, the church focused on a few priority activities (2:42). First, the believers understood the high level of commitment to 'the apostles' teaching'. They wanted and needed to know the mind and will of God in their new-found faith. By this means they were grounded in the fundamentals. Much later, this solid biblical foundation would serve them well when they dealt with tough issues such as those encountered in the Jerusalem Council (15:1-29).

Second, they sought fellowship around the breaking of bread. These would be times of sharing their common faith and food. The primary emphasis here seems to be on the mealtime, not on the Lord's Supper. Grammatically, 'fellowship' and 'the breaking of bread' are linked to describe one activity, not two.

Third, they understood their utter dependence on God in prayer. So we are not surprised to find this at the top of their priority list. Nor are we amazed to see how closely these three activities correspond to the priorities of the apostles as spoken of later (Acts 6:4).

This does not mean that the church did nothing else. However, it does mean that these were the most important and the most regularly practised.

Strong Spiritual Leadership

It did not take long for the scope of ministry to exceed the time and energy of the apostles. They needed additional help so that they could keep their focus on prayer and the Word (6:4) while other equally important aspects of ministry were not neglected, such as caring for widows (6:1-2).

But not just any willing person qualified to help. Consider the extremely high standard for leadership set by the apostles for those who would serve the widows.

'But select from among you, brethren, seven men of good reputation, full of the Spirit and of wisdom, whom we may put in charge of this task' (6:3).

Spiritual service demands high spiritual qualifying standards. The first church received these qualifications from the Apostles. Paul would later elaborate on the details (1 Timothy 3:1-13; Titus 1:5-9).

An Uncommon Concern For One Another

One of the striking features of the Jerusalem church was the 'one mindedness' of the believers. Whether in prayer (1:14; 4:24), worship (5:12), decision making (15:25) or just living out the Christian life (2:46), they were of one mind.

This translated into a wonderful feature of the church. They possessed an uncommon preoccupation with the welfare of one another.

And all those who had believed were together, and had all things in common; and they began selling their property and possessions, and were sharing them with all, as anyone might have need. And day by day continuing with one mind in the temple, and breaking bread from house to house, they were taking their meals together with gladness and sincerity of heart (Acts 2:44-46).

And the congregation of those who believed were of one heart and soul; and not one of them claimed that anything belonging to him was his own; but all things were common property to them. And with great power the apostles were giving witness to the resurrection of the Lord Jesus, and abundant grace was upon them all. For there was not a needy person among them, for all who were owners of land or houses would sell them and bring the proceeds of the sales, and lay them at the apostles' feet; and they would be distributed to each, as any had need (Acts 4:32-35).

The level of sacrifice in caring for one another seemed to be in proportion to the abundant grace that was upon them all (4:33). They lived out Christ's pronouncement, 'By this all men will know that you are My disciples, if you have love one for another' (John 13:35).

Paul would later urge the Roman church to embrace this same kind of unity.

Now may the God who gives perseverance and encouragement grant you to be of the same mind with one another according to Christ Jesus; that with one accord you may with one voice glorify the God and Father of our Lord Jesus Christ (Romans 15:5-6).

The First Church

Because of the unique significance of this inaugural assembly, let's summarize the major features in order to appreciate the superlative qualities of the Jerusalem church built by God. The first church was characterized by:

1. A high view of Scripture
2. Reliance on the Holy Spirit
3. The discipline of prayer
4. Bold evangelism
5. Church growth
6. A high standard of commitment
7. Willingness to sacrifice
8. A 'Great Commission' orientation
9. Well defined priorities

10. Strong spiritual leadership
11. An uncommon concern for one another

For those today who still question what the church should be and do, let me point them to the church at Jerusalem as a starting place in finding their answer. Christ commends these features to the contemporary church just as He applauded them in 'the first church'.

POSTSCRIPT

'What Would Christ Say About Your Church?'

Maybe by now you are asking, 'So what? How can I use this material?'

Please realize that these first century messages apply directly to twentieth century churches all over the world. They rise above time and culture. The observations and conclusions compiled for each church did not come from human wisdom but rather by divine inspiration since they came directly from the Bible. They explicitly define, from Christ's perspective, what the church should actually be and do.

The results of our study have not taken the form of theory but rather practice. We do know what Christ thinks about His church. We do have the mind of Christ (1 Corinthians 2:16). We now need to apply these things to our churches.

God's Word has preserved for us these particular timeless qualities that He commends for the church and these that He condemns. Taken together, they serve as a sort of 'plumbline' to measure and compare the current reality in your church against the perfect standards that Christ has set down for His bride, the church.

Every pastor, every elder, even every Christian should take time to contemplate this one overarching question: *'If Jesus Christ were to write my church a letter, like He wrote in Scripture, what would He say?'* What would he commend? What would He tell you to add that is currently not in the church? What would He condemn? What would He insist that the church never embrace because it is condemnable?

To help you answer these questions in a meaningful way, I have compiled the major commendable and condemnable features discovered in the twelve churches under examination. You can meaningfully evaluate your own church by identifying those features, both commendable and condemnable, that characterize your church.

The following abbreviations will help you relate these features back to the individual churches in our study for a fuller consideration of each one.

Ephesus (E)
Smyrna (S)
Pergamum (P)
Thyatira (TY)
Sardis (SA)
Philadelphia (PA)
Laodicea (L)
Thessalonica (TH)
Philippi (PI)
Corinth (C)
Antioch (A)
Jerusalem (J)

COMMENDABLE FEATURES
Good deeds (E, TY, TH)
Hard work (E, TH)
Endurance (E, TY, PA, TH)
Discernment (E, A)
Suffering (S, TH, J)
Faithfulness to the end (S)
Holding fast to Christ's name (P, PA)
Not denying the faith (P, J)
Love (TY)
Faith (TY)
Service (TY, TH)

Righteous life (SA)
Keeping Christ's Word (PA)
Submitting (TH)
Reproducing (TH, A, J)
Repentance (TH)
Patience (TH)
Accepting God's Word (TH, A, J)
Standing firm (TH, C)
Pleasing God (TH)
Loving the brethren (TH, J)
Prayer (TH, PI, C, J)
Evangelistic fervour (PI, A, J)
Baptismal emphasis (PI, J)
Strong teaching/preaching (PI, C, A, J)
Spiritual leadership (PI, A, J)
Dependence on God (PI)
Joyful attitudes (PI)
Generosity (PI, A, J)
Boldness (A, J)
Growth (A, J)
Ministry of the Holy Spirit (A, J)
Discipleship (A)
Sacrifice (S, J)
Spiritual priorities (J)
Spiritual potential (C)
Submission to God's sovereignty (S, P, PI)
True worship (J)

CONDEMNABLE FEATURES

Lost love (E)
Absence of first deeds (E)
Compromise (P)
Tolerating sin (TY, C)
Immorality (P, TY, C)
Idolatry (P, TY)

Deadness (SA)

Incomplete deeds (SA)

Lukewarmness (L)

Hypocrisy (L)

False teaching (P, TY, TH, PI, C)

Undisciplined living (TH)

Disunity (PI)

Sin (J, C)

Arrogant divisions (C)

Prolonged spiritual immaturity (C)

Sueing one another (C)

Abusing Christian liberty (C)

Profaning the Lord's Supper (C)

Misappropriating spiritual gifts (C)

Unwillingness to forgive (C)

Slow to give (C)

Critical of leadership (C)

Use the Evaluation Worksheet (page 218) provided to construct the present profile of your church. The result should be a close approximation of what Jesus would say if He were to write a letter to your church, because that is what He said when He wrote in the first century.

Now, as you engage in preserving, remodelling, and even rebuilding your church according to Christ's biblical expectations, I pray that you will do so with the same attitude of that third workman on Sir Christopher Wren's building project, St. Paul's Cathedral. Commit yourself today to be part of a magnificent effort to build Christ's church worldwide to the glory of God.

QUESTIONS FOR FURTHER REFLECTION

1. Which first century church best describes your church?

2. What qualities would Christ commend in your church?

3. What commendable features would Christ have you add that are not now current characteristics?

4. What would Christ condemn in your church?

5. What minor situations would Christ have your church abandon now, before these situations expand and bring Christ's condemnation later?

6. Whose responsibility is it to take corrective action in the church?

7. Is God's Word the only blueprint your church will use to build and remodel?

8. Is your church's chief purpose to glorify God through the building of Christ's church?

9. Are you praying that Christ will change your church to be more pleasing to Himself?

10. What can you do to assist the process?

EVALUATION WORKSHEET

*'If Jesus Christ were to write my church a letter,
like those He wrote in Scripture, what would He say?'*

COMMENDABLE FEATURES	CONDEMNABLE FEATURES
1.	1.
2.	2.
3.	3.
4.	4.
5.	5.
6.	6.
7.	7.
8.	8.
9.	9.
10.	10.
11.	11.
12.	12.
13.	13.
14.	14.
15.	15.

HELPFUL READING

I. THE CHURCHES OF ASIA

William Barclay. *Letters to the Seven Churches*. London: SCM, 1957.

Colin J. Hemer. *The Letters to the Seven Churches of Asia in their Local Setting*. Sheffield: JSOT, 1986.

Stephen J. Lawson. *Final Call*. Wheaton, IL: Crossway, 1994.

Robert Murray M'Cheyne. *The Seven Churches of Asia*. Ross-Shire, Scotland: Christian Focus, rpt, 1986.

G. Campbell Morgan. *A First Century Message to Twentieth Century Christians*. New York: Revell, 1902.

William Ramsay. *The Letters to the Seven Churches*. Minneapolis: James Family, rpt. 1978.

John R. W. Stott. *What Christ Thinks of the Church*. Grand Rapids: Eerdmans, 1958.

II. THE CHURCHES OF GREECE

Thessalonica

D. Edmond Hiebert. *The Thessalonian Epistles*. Chicago: Moody, 1971.

Robert Thomas. "The Thessalonian Epistles," in *Expositor's Bible Commentary*, vol. 11, ed. Frank Gaebelein. Grand Rapids: Zondervan, 1978.

Philippi

William Hendrikson. *Exposition of Philippians*. Grand Rapids: Baker, 1961.

Homer A. Kent, Jr. "Philippians" in *Expositor's Bible Commentary*, vol. 11, ed. Frank Gaebelein. Grand Rapids: Zondervan, 1978.

John B. Lightfoot. *Commentary on the Epistle of St. Paul to the Philippians*. Grand Rapids: Zondervan, rpt. 1953.

Corinth

Gordon H. Fee. *The First Epistle to the Corinthians* (NICNT). Grand Rapids: Eerdmans, 1987.

Harold Mare. "I Corinthians," in *Expositor's Bible Commentary*, vol. 10, ed. Frank Gaebelein. Grand Rapids: Zondervan, 1976.

Philip E. Hughes. *Commentary on the Second Epistle to the Corinthians* (NICNT). Grand Rapids: Eerdmans, 1962.

Homer A. Kent, Jr, *A Heart Opened Wide*. Grand Rapids: Baker, 182.

III. THE CHURCHES OF THE EAST

F.F. Bruce. *The Book of the Acts* (NICNT). Grand Rapids: Eerdmans , 1988.

Homer A. Kent, Jr. *Jerusalem to Rome, Studies in Acts*. Grand Rapids: Baker, 1977.

Richard N. Longenecker. "The Acts of the Apostles," in *Expositor's Bible Commentary*, vol. 9, ed. Frank Gaebelein. Grand Rapids: Zondervan, 1981.

ENDNOTES

Introduction—"I Will Build My Church"
1. John Seel, *The Evangelical Forfeit* (Grand Rapids: Baker, 1993) 48-65.
2. Author unknown.

Chapter Three—Smyrna: The Suffering Church
1. Marie G. King, ed., *Foxe's Book of Martyrs* (Old Tappan, NJ: Revell, 1968) 13,15.
2. William Barclay, *The Revelation of John*, vol.1 (Philadelphia: Westminster, 1976) 76-77.

Chapter Four—Pergamum: The Compromising Church
1. Mrs. Howard Taylor, "Whether by Life or by Death," *Moody Monthly* (December 1984) 120-121.

Chapter Seven—Philadelphia: The Obedient Church
1. For a more detailed discussion of the rapture please see my *Snatched Before the Storm: A Case for Pretribulationism,* (Winona Lake, IN: BMH Books, 1979).

Chapter Ten—Philippi: The Caring Church
1. Polycarp, "The Epistle of S. Polycarp" in *The Apostolic Fathers*, ed. by J.B. Lightfoot (Grand Rapids: Baker, rpt. 1976) 96.

Chapter Twelve—Antioch: The Sending Church
1. Dallas Willard, "Discipleship for Super-Christians Only?" *Christianity Today* (October 10, 1980) 23.

SCRIPTURE INDEX

OLD TESTAMENT

NEW TESTAMENT

STUDY GUIDE

Questions For Revelation 1-3

1. What practical significance does each feature of Christ's appearance have for you and your church (Revelation 1:14-16)?

2. What encouragement does each appeal of Christ have for you (Revelation 1:17-18)?

3. Consider how you personally and your church corporately would be evaluated by Christ according to the Scriptures in regard to the ten broad implications listed on page 40.

4. Are you giving your best (100%) to Christ in the church?

Questions For Ephesus: Revelation 2:1-7

1. What do you know about the Ephesian church from other Scriptures (see Acts 18-20; Ephesians; 1 Timothy 1:3)?

2. What significance did the symbols used of Christ have for the Ephesians (2:1)?

3. What did Christ find to commend in the Ephesian church (2:2-3, 6)?

4. Who were the Nicolaitans (2:6)?

5. What 'first love' had the Ephesians left (2:4; see John 14-16)?

6. To what 'first deeds' did the Ephesians need to return (2:5)?

7. How does the Ephesian letter relate to your church?

Questions For Smyrna: Revelation 2:8-11

1. What do you know about Smyrna from church history?

2. What was the significance to those in Smyrna of the descriptions used of Christ (2:8)?

3. What did Christ find to commend in the Smyrna church (2:9)?

4. What is the 'synagogue of Satan' (2:9; cf. 3:9)?

5. How is the church to face persecution (2:10)?

6. What is promised to the faithful church (2:10-11)?

7. What twentieth century churches have had parallel experiences to the Smyrna church?

Questions For Pergamum: Revelation 2:12-17

1. What do you know about Pergamum from history (2:12)?

2. What was the significance to those in Pergamum of the descriptions used of Christ (2:12)?

3. What did Christ find commendable in the Pergamum church (2:13)?

4. What is the 'throne of Satan' (2:13)?

5. What did Christ have against the church (2:14-15)?

6. What was the 'teaching of Balaam' (2:14)?

7. Why and how will Christ make war with the Pergamum church (2:16)?

8. What is promised to the overcomers (2:17)?

9. What kind of 20th century churches deserve the same sort of condemnation as Pergamum received?

Questions for Thyatira: Revelation 2:18-29

1. What is the significance of the symbols used for Christ (Revelation 2:18)?

2. What did Christ find commendable in the Thyatira church (Revelation 2:19)?

3. What is the teaching of Jezebel (Revelation 2:20)?

4. What is God's judgement for failing to repent (Revelation 2:21-23)?

5. What are Satan's so-called deep secrets (Revelation 2:24)?

6. What does Christ demand of the saints at Thyatira (Revelation 2:25)?

7. What does Christ promise to those who obey (2:26-28)?

Questions for Sardis: Revelation 3:1-6

1. Who or what are the 'seven spirits' (3:1)?

2. How can a church be alive and dead at the same time (3:1)?

3. What characterizes a church that is asleep (3:2-3)?

4. In what way will Jesus come to Sardis (3:3)?

5. What are the 'soiled clothes' in the Christian life (3:4)?

6. What does 'dressed in white' mean (3:5)?

7. Can a Christian have his or her name blotted out of the Lamb's book of life (3:5)?

Questions For Philadelphia: Revelation 3:7-13

1.   What is the significance of the symbols used for Christ (3:7)?

2.   What did Christ find commendable in the Philadelphian church (3:8)?

3.   Whom does Christ call 'of the synagogue of Satan' (3:9)?

4.   What is the 'hour of testing' and to whom does it apply (3:10)?

5.   What is the significance of Christ's warning (3:11)?

6.   What does Christ promise to those who will obey (3:12)?

7.   What will be Christ's 'new name' (3:12)?

Questions for Laodicea: Revelation 3:14-22

1. What do Christ's introductory descriptions represent (3:14)?

2. What do 'lukewarm', 'hot', and 'cold' mean (3:15-16)?

3. How will Christ spit the church out of His mouth (3:16)?

4. What was wrong with Laodicea's self-image (3:17)?

5. What does God prescribe for spiritual recovery (3:18)?

6. Does 3:19-20 refer to salvation or to the restoration of sinning believers?

7. How will the Father, the Son and all believers occupy the throne of heaven together (3:21)?

Questions About The Thessalonian Church

1. Under what kind of conditions did the church begin and grow?

2. How important was the Word of God in the church?

3. After they were saved, what kind of a response did the Thessalonians have to their preconversion lives?

4. In what way did the church respond to Christ's Great Commission?

5. How did the church respond to Christ's authority in the church?

6. What role did faith, love and hope play in the church?

7. For what reasons did the church seem to mature so rapidly?

8. How do the positive qualities of the church corporately apply to you individually?

Questions About The Philippian Church

1. What kind of a plan did Paul use to plant the Philippian church?

2. Under what conditions did the Philippian church begin?

3. Why did the Philippians place so much importance on their Great Commission ministry?

4. What leadership pattern does the Book of Philippians exhibit?

5. How generous were the Philippian believers?

6. What dangers did the church face?

7. How can your church be impacted by adopting the Philippian pattern?

Questions About The Corinthian Church

1.   How does Corinth compare to the churches at Ephesus, Pergamum and Thyatira?

2.   What commendable features did Paul compliment?

3.   Why was Paul afraid for the Corinthian church?

4. What attitude did the Corinthians display towards spiritual leadership?

5.   What one attitude summarizes all of the condemnable features of Corinth?

6.   If the Corinthian church were to be revived, where would it start?

7.   How could such a blessed church be so immature and subject to such condemnation?

Questions About The Antiochan Church

1.   What caused the boldness of the believers in Antioch?

2.   How did numerical growth occur in Antioch?

3.   What priority level did preaching and teaching assume in the church?

4.   Why were the brethren at Antioch so generous?

5.   What can your church learn from the outreach ministry of Antioch?

6.   How important did doctrinal discernment become to the church?

7.   Why was Antioch such a strategic location for a church?

Questions About The Jerusalem Church

1. How did the Jerusalem church approach Scripture?

2. What role did prayer play in church life?

3. Why were the Christians so bold in their evangelism?

4. What kind of a harvest did Jerusalem have as a result of their ministry approach?

5. How committed were they to the Great Commission mandates?

6. What activities had the highest priority in the church?

7. How did believers in Jerusalem treat each other?